INVISIBLE
GRANDPARENTING

Leave a Legacy of Love
Whether You Can Be There or Not

Pat Hanson, Ph.D

PARK PLACE PUBLICATIONS
PACIFIC GROVE, CALIFORNIA

Invisible Grandparenting: Leave a Legacy of Love
Whether You Can Be There or Not
Pat Hanson, Ph.D

Published by
Park Place Publications
Pacific Grove, California
www.parkplacepublications.com

ISBN: 978-1-935530-83-1

Cover design by Larry Kingsland (www.pivotal-design.com)
Book design and format by Patricia Hamilton

Printed in U.S.A.

First U.S. Edition: October 2013

CONTENTS

Acknowledgments   VII

INTRODUCTION 1
Who We Are   3
Overview   5

• ❖ •

MY BACK-STORY: FROM CHILDLESS MOM
TO INVISIBLE GRANDPARENT 9
Two Sides to Every Story and Then the Truth   9
  Part One: Kicking and Screaming into
            Accidental Grandparenting   11
  Part Two: Deeper into Invisibility   20
  Part Three: Writing Letters Helps Heal Hurt   27

Update Twelve Years Later—Heart-full-ness!   33

• ❖ •

HANDLING INVISIBILITY 37
How We Cope   37
The Interviews   39
  Darrie: Early Memories from Therapy
    Lead to Accusations   39
  Shawna: Addictions and the Courts
    Complicate the Situation   40
  Alia: A Metaphysical Perspective   43
  Roxanne: A Therapist's Personal Challenge   45
  Gloria: From Pain to Advocacy   48
  Chelsea: Invisible Auntie   52

CONTENTS (CONTINUED)

INVISIBLE BUT NOT SILENT:
LETTER WRITING AS A HEALING TOOL 57
What in Your Bones Do You Want
    Your Grandchildren to Know?   58
Writing Letters to Save and Share Someday (SSS Letters)   59
Writing Said but Never Send (SNS) Letters   60
Release: Transform Negative Energy to Forgiveness   65

⊡ ⊞ ⊡

MY LEGACY OF LETTERS AND LIFE LESSONS 69
My Invisibility Continued   70
Out of Sight, Out of Mind? Not Really.   70
Partially Visible Grandparenting Can Hurt Too   73
Watch out for Expectations   76
Your Father Showed Up!   78
Your Father Called Today   79
Oh the Places We Would Go!   81
Postcard Memories: Santa Barbara   81
Birthday I.O.U.'s   83
A Christmas Trip to Radio City NYC   85
Spike Jonze's Where The Wild Things Are—Too Wild?   87
Sleeping Beauty—Out of Date?   89
Love, Sex and Marriage   91
You Were Married Three Times, Grandma. Why?   91
Valentine's Days Are Difficult   97
From Maiden to Mother to Crone   99
Family Issues   101
Great Grandma Wilkin's Memoir-ies   101
Why Do Holidays Bring Out Family Dysfunction?   106
Compulsive Cleaning? OCD? Or Just Chores?   109

Tips for Getting Along In Life   111
  Watch Your Language   *111*
  My Broken Listener   *112*
  Thank-you's Are Important   *114*
  Go On With the Show   *116*

Peace and Politics   118
  Arlington West: Veterans for Peace Memorial   *118*
  The Election: A Not Impossible Dream   *120*
  The Election Is Over. Wear Purple!   *122*

Church, God and Spirituality   125
  Gentle with Myself   *125*
  A Baby Blessing   *127*
  February 22nd, Twenty-ten Love Train!   *129*
  Easter as Resurrection Day   *132*

Aging, Dying and Death   134
  Gettin' Old   *134*
  Saying Good-Bye   *136*
  Death   *139*
  A Military Funeral   *142*

HEALING   145
Separation: A Most Dificult Challenge   145
The Only Way Out Is Through   146
What a Great Grandparent You Would Be!   147
Find Something to be Grateful For   148
Forgiveness Is Not the Final Frontier   150
And Finally, Grandmother Yourself!   150

AN ELEVATED EPILOGUE   155
APPENDIX AND RESOURCES   159

ACKNOWLEDGMENTS

Buckets of appreciation go to the many friends and professionals in the publishing industry who have listened to "my story" for over a decade and encouraged me to articulate it, not only for my own clarity, but also for others. My first appreciation goes to my still breathing 93-year-old mother, without whose criticism of my writing that began in my early school years and continued till her dementia, I may never have become the writer I am. I also thank her for the financial support that made publication of this first sample of "my voice" possible.

My second thank–you goes to Lily, who as you will read, became the mother at sixteen of my first grandchild. She literally gave me the idea for writing letters and saving them, and read this entire manuscript. Martha Drexler Osler read my first rather self-righteous ramblings and cautioned me to stretch beyond the anger, pointing me towards the healing that indeed took place. Ann Todd Jealous, my therapist of ten years, witnessed my journey and was the first to let me know I was not alone in losing access to grandchildren. Without the influence of Reverend Deborah L. Johnson and the spiritual principles of Inner Light Ministries about healing separation, my own evolution and this text may never have manifested.

For five years, Writers Circles led by Elin Kelsey, and two years of Ellen Bass's weekly "Writing for Our Lives" sessions, provided essential feedback as themes developed. I can still hear my writing partner, Dick Guthrie of "Gone to Soldiers, Every One," clamoring for more structure. I trust you will find it here.

Following my winning third in David Henry Sterry and Arielle Eckstut's first Pitchapalooza in 2010, their subsequent feedback as www.thebookdoctors.com guided me to this final draft. Just because she believed in this work, Stephanie Pearly spent dozens of hours gratis, meticulously grooming the first book proposal and its sample chapters, as did Gwyn Weger and Tanya Lawrence on later editions. Finally, it was a delight to renew memories of a friendship that began 40+ years ago, as Bernie Borok provided the final professional proofread.

And last but not least, I thank my husband and "significant equal," Larry Kingsland, for his patience, constant support, encouragement, advice, and the creative design of my website, but most of all for believing in me. Many others influenced this book from inception of idea to these final electronic and printed words. They know who they are, even if I've forgotten to name some. Namasté to you all.

Pat Hanson, August 30, 2013

INTRODUCTION

When our memories are all we have,
why are some of us kept from having some?

The dictionary defines "invisibility" as something impossible to see, unseen, imperceptible, hidden, imaginary, made transparent magically, or unrecorded statistically and therefore undetectable. For far too many of us, that involves grandchildren, or nephews and nieces. For me it involves a granddaughter almost eleven I have been kept from seeing, by circumstances out of my control, since she was four. I can count on my hands the number of times I visited a thirteen-year-old grandson. Then I was often among a group of elder relatives, but only recently seen as "grandma."

LETTER #1
August 20, 2008*
Dear Annie:
    You will be having your first day of school sometime this week!
    That must be exciting! Or is it scary? How would you describe it to me? Would you call and tell me? Or send me pictures? I would really REALLY love that.
    I still have a photo of your father (your biological father, not John who is doing such a wonderful job of being a dad to you) getting on a big yellow school bus in 1986. He was as handsome and proud as you are beautiful.
    "What's 'bio-log-i-cal father' mean?"
    It means that when you were born you came part from your mother and part from my son, Brad, the dad you knew for a while when you were a baby and then some weekends till you were four. He went away two years ago on what I hope is his "low road to enlightenment" because he had a drug problem, and did not get along with your mom.

"What's en-light-en-ment?"

Good question: I think it's finding peace (being happy) with yourself and the world and your place in it. It has a lot to do with "God" but we don't need to talk about that right now. We'll do it in some other letter.

So your father disappearing does not mean that he doesn't love you. Or that he doesn't love me, his mom. He always did; nor do I love him any less for making some bad choices. Somehow it was meant for you to be raised by your mom and John, and to have your wonderful sister. And for some reason that I have yet to understand, it was meant right now for me not to be in your life in person. Your mom wants to erase the memory of your former father from your life, and when you moved, she refused to give me your address or phone number. I can't even get it from your other grandparents.

Oh well. I get to love you and envision you growing up safe and sound and happy and getting all the things you deserve in life … invisibly. I am the Grandma you may not see for a long long time, or ever again. But I will be watching over you from a distance, and sending good thoughts every single day.

I am going to write these letters to you and save them. Someday when you're grown up you may decide to look me up. A very big pile of letters will be waiting for you.

I decided to write to you because it is a way for me to participate in your life on some level. It also should help heal the hole in my heart from not being able to see you and play with you. It fills the time I now have at sixty-three to come and babysit, or help you with your homework, or take you to parks and zoos and theatre and concerts. Time that could have given your dad and very very good mom a break. I get only to imagine doing that.

This is a lot for one day, before you even go to school for the first time. I can't wait till you can really learn how

to read well! I know you've started already.
Just know I love you, and that you will feel this love
deep in your heart whether you know it or not.
LOVE,
Your "Invisible Grandma" Pat
P. S. I hope you get a great great kindergarten teacher.

*Note: All names except my own have been changed.

The letter you just witnessed is one among hundreds that I have written and am saving in hopes that someday Annie, who is part of my gene pool and looks just like I did at her age, will read them. The last time I saw her she was four. Seven years! Seven missed Valentine's Days, seven Easters, seven Halloweens and the hardest: seven Mother's Days!

Over the past decade I only got to imagine Annie or Carter excited to see me, running to my open arms spouting versions of "Gam-ma" that become more and more articulate as they get older. There is an empty spot on my counter every year for Christmas cards I'll never get, or thank-you notes signed in their developing handwriting for birthday presents I can't send.

I don't know whether its post-menopausal serenity without the rolling hormones, or my own mortality peeking around the corner, with its hand thumbing my face, but now when I finally found myself ready to enjoy the loving part of the grandparenting process that my peers rave so much about, I wasn't able do it. Now that I want to contribute to budding personalities that are my own grandchildren, I cannot.

Who We Are

In 2008 at a storytelling in a national conference of older women in Seattle, I first told my "Invisible Grandparent" tale from the stage to 400 women. Afterwards at least two dozen came up to me saying, "That's my story too." Each bared her own kind of grief. Their reasons differed. Several were lesbian couples, some had religious or political differences between themselves and their children's families, others mentioned issues ranging from personality and control issues to geographic separation. A few bared the pain they felt when as addictions took over, their children became different people from the child they had raised.

As I continued to air my own grief in public, I realized how much residual secrecy, resentment and shame is out there. There is an enormous need for a vehicle for healing all types of invisibility and separation. Like me you may be partially visible and have tangible memories and ideas of where your grandchildren are, and what they look like, having once played a role in a young one's life and then were blocked from it. Or, you may not even know your grandchildren's whereabouts or even their names.

There are millions of us who, because of personality conflicts, our children's long-distance careers, divorce and complicated custody issues, consequences of addictions or even choices made long ago about adoption and abortion, cannot see our grandkids as much as they would like and might want to pass on our values and memories.

There are all kinds of adult-child intergenerational invisibility. Recently, a friend's first-expected grandchild very unexpectedly ended up stillborn at full term. The grief I saw on her face while she sat at a choir concert as if nothing had happened was palpable. I have another friend who gave a child up for adoption forty years ago during the Vietnam War. To this day she wonders if the teenagers she runs into in her hometown are the by-product of her never-forgotten act. Another quite privileged friend confided in me that she was an invisible Auntie. For seven years a clash with her sister has blocked her from seeing a nephew and niece she'd been close to, and had even written into her will.

We are all invisible grandparents, whether we realize it or not. Most of us will be long gone by the time our grandchildren, likely adults by then, ask questions about us, i.e, what we were like, or what psychic or genetic imprint we may have made on their lives.

A friend my age, also born in 1945, who recently became a

grandmother herself, only now started wondering what her own grandmother, who died in 1955 when she was ten, was really like. All she remembers is the woman in her family photos wearing a long black dress and sourpuss face. She was sorry she couldn't remember if she'd asked her any questions at all.

Overview

This book explores the many steps, both healthy and ungracious, that people have taken to cope with circumstances that have placed them where they can only imagine the growth of their grandchildren. The tools in *Invisible Grandparenting* give us a safe way to revisit situations we may have kept shrouded in mystery.

In *My Back-Story*, I tell my version of the circumstances that led to my status as an invisible grandparent.

In *Handling Invisibility*, others like me share their stories of how they handled their situation.

In *Invisible Not Silent* I show how letter writing can be a healing tool, as well as a means to communicate the gifts, tangible and intangible, that grandparents might like to pass on, if they could. Writing can help us clarify our feelings and can be a healing vehicle for those not able to pass on firsthand the love they might care to. Also, by writing inevitable feelings of frustration, anger and even outrage out in letters never intended for sharing, and specifically designed for release, one can begin to transform negative energy to forgiveness. Some things can be changed from obstacles to opportunities, and perhaps even be seen as cosmic destiny for you to learn from in this lifetime.

My Legacy in Letters is a sample of the many kinds of letters I've written since 2008. It also contains "Life Lessons" that I would like to pass on. A legacy is something from the past bequeathed to younger generations. It is something left behind to immortalize us; something that keeps the past alive for many future "presents." For some it may be writing: journals, a book, poetry or letters.

For others it may be scrapbooks of family photos and recipes. Artwork or jewelry often is passed on generation to generation. Actual memories of people's lives may end up as "stories" bordering on "tall tales," retold over and over and over again to the point of turning into legends. For me it was the letters and "Life Lessons" I am sharing with you.

Healing is about recovering emotionally or spiritually from separation of all kinds. It details what I did to feel my feelings, and not spiral down to the helplessness of depression. It reminds us to rise above the drama of our own personal predicament. By finding something to be grateful for every day, and forgiving ourselves we can get through the most trying situations. This chapter helps us envision, hold high aspirations for our young ones, and believe them, so that a positive vibration is transmitted to the universe. Not an easy task under difficult circumstances, but it will start us on that path.

In the *Appendix* you will find a list of resources to turn to for help. There are numerous organizations for grandparents in need of personal support and legal advice. There are also many ways we can, if we choose, give service to young children other than our own grandkids needing positive role models. It is a mere sampling of the many support groups and services available to estranged families.

And finally, *Grandmother Yourself* reminds us to take care of ourselves. Who among us has not wished for a soothing voice, or a warm lap to drop into, not only when things are tough, but also when we have precious joys to share? By being gentle with and taking care of ourselves, we will discover that our first and foremost contribution to the planet is just that: our selves.

You are not alone. You can, right now, find a way to leave your own particular legacy behind whether you can be there or not. Let's do it.

MY BACK-STORY: FROM CHILDLESS MOM TO INVISIBLE GRANDPARENT

Two Sides to Every Story and Then the Truth

I must admit that I went kicking and screaming into accepting my own aging and the fact I could achieve grandparent status. In my early 50s, I was plenty old enough. Born in 1945, a hair too old to be an official baby boomer, I wasn't ready for the stereotypical ubiquitous silver-haired old lady designation.

Yet today I realize how important it is that kids get to know adult role models other than, and older than, their own parents. Moms and dads are often too strung out from the 24/7 exhaustion and stress of parenting and working to do it well all by themselves. They need help with bedtime stories, picking kids up from school, helping with homework, not to mention ventures to museums, excursions to other neighborhoods, exposure to different cultures … all the things most grandparents are willing and able to do.

What has kept me from doing these things? What forces contrived to keep me from doing the intergenerational educating I now was ready to be doing? The truth. My particular truths are difficult to admit, but I had to speak them aloud to help me heal my feelings around the circumstances that created my invisibility.

My first particular truth is that in 1999, in spite of my being a lifelong sex educator, my risk-taking, 17-year-old firstborn son Brad, who'd had access to condoms since the 5th grade, got his 16-year-old first-ever real girlfriend pregnant. He then became too afraid of himself to stick around, and escaped his situation in any way he could. First with alcohol, then pot, and finally with many broken promises. Just before his son was born, he moved from New York to California.

The second unalterable truth is that he did it again two years later! This time with a bright, lovely, perky girl he'd met after I'd kicked him out of my own home when he was 20.

Thank the goddess, the true story that follows is that the two wonderful young women to whom my son was drawn (Lily, mother of Carter, now 13; and Suzie, mother of Annie, now 11), had the emotional intelligence to leave my then bad boy behind, and become the loving mothers they are. With the help of other more stable young men who loved and married them, they have each begotten a second and third child. My son's journey, while he took us down roads no parent ever wants to traverse, has a happy ending too. Stay tuned.

Both of these new families have a full set of grandparents. What is hard for me in both cases, one more painful than the other because it is a girl who is a cookie-cutter image of me at that age, is that I get to be invisible. I don't count. In my case, the difficulty of telling children at a young age (or any age, for that matter) the honest story about their lineage has wiped out any feelings of empathy or obligation on the part of that grandchild's biological mother. That is the proverbial long story made short. I may never know the truth.

Besides being hurt and perplexed when first confronted with the fact that I was being cut out of the life of the darling bright blonde brown-eyed four-year-old girl who I'd held at birth and had last played dress-up with in my own stairwell, I was pissed. I could somewhat understand that her mom might want to erase every memory of my son's bad behavior in those few years from her daughter's memory bank, but why me also? What had I done but visit monthly when she had allowed it?

Yet, the other of these two beautiful young mothers, Lily, suggested a way to heal the separation that absolutely opened my heart at this pivotal stage in my own life. Writing letters for over four years as an invisible grandparent to the children I don't get to see as often as I'd like, has enabled me to get over my own resentment and guilt. Saving them has helped me leave a legacy of love whether I can be there or not.

Releasing others that I wrote, never to be sent, helped me get beyond the disappointment that escalated into anger, rage and pain that came as a result of this separation. It is my fervent hope that others reading this will do the same.

The backstory that follows will illuminate my version of what happened. But as my minister says, "There are at least two sides to every story, and then there's the truth." What you read here is merely my perception of the events that occurred in the last 12 years. Please remember that all names have been changed except my own.

Part One: Kicking and Screaming into Accidental Grandparenting

For years, near the end of my forties, I'd wince and come close to gagging whenever someone said to me, "I can't wait to be a grandparent!" When both men and women donned a beatific smile and went "go goo-goo ga-ga" in the presence of a tiny baby, losing any semblance of an articulate mind, I'd bite my tongue and paint a poker face rather than show my personal sense of disapproval that bordered on disgust. As people dragged out baby pictures in business meetings, I'd suddenly have to leave the room to go to the bathroom or get coffee. Today I am getting closer to understanding what was behind this for me.

"Just wait and see," a few close friends said. "You love your own children involuntarily. Yes. But it becomes a whole different ballgame when they're your grandchildren. It's even deeper."

"Thank you, I prefer to wait," I would say, shrugging. At the time it wasn't quite clear to me where the shiver of my reluctance to openly admit that I was both old enough and wise enough to be a grandmother came from. Perhaps it was a premonition of the way it would slap me in the face a few years later.

I have always been labeled a maverick, first in 1964 when I balked at teaching only cooking and sewing with my degree in Home Economics. I brought boys into my high school classroom and taught family life and sex education before the John Birch Society called it a "communist plot." I even had a child development lab built, so these teenagers could peek at what many of them would be doing all too soon after graduation.

Divorced and remarried by the time I was 34 wasn't too out of the ordinary; nor was being labeled an "elderly prime-ep" (first-time mother) in the hospital when at 36 and 38, I had the two blonde, brown-eyed boys I always knew I would. Splitting from their dad when they were two and four, because all the therapy we'd pursued pointed to how we didn't actually like one another, much less could survive parenting under the same roof, wasn't too uncommon either. By 1986 many women were seeing the writing on the wall and getting out of bad marriages far earlier than their foremothers had.

After a year of shuffling kids between two houses a mile apart, I was offered a dream job 3,000 miles away. With my ex's blessing, I took it and we agreed on a bi-coastal custody arrangement. That was radical. I paid child support nine months a year. Our kids spent summers and school vacations in California, living the stable school year in New York with their dad and his new wife.

At the time of the divorce my ex and I had declared we wanted to provide a model of a loving relationship for our boys that wasn't possible between us. Within months of our separation, with difficulty, considerable help from my friends, and multiple therapies, I had to accept just that. "Women mourn and men replace," I told myself. Julie, the "cookie baker," became my ex's second wife and fell into the role of my kids' stepmom, scout leader, and Pop Warner football coach with an ease I never could have.

Over the years I got used to the idea. One Christmas day I even wrote a letter to Newsweek's MY TURN, ostensibly thanking Julie for her up-close parenting, declaring, *Stepmom Is Not a Dirty Word.*"

Co-parenting in this manner generally turned out well. However, on the eve of my firstborn's high school graduation, I found myself in a therapist's office with him, not quite ready for another bump in the roller coaster ride my headstrong adolescent son had already given us that spring.

My 17-year-old, blonde, brown-eyed, 6-foot-1, movie-star-gorgeous son had muscular six-pack abs, and got in the 85th percentile on his SATs (that he probably took stoned), and looked like something from a Ralph Lauren ad in the Sunday *New York Times*. He was seeing a shrink his live-in father and I, his long-distance mom, had arranged. He'd gotten a DUI (actually for driving under the influence of controlled substances: pot), on the eve of his coming to California that May. That weekend he was supposed to both register for community college and take a local girl he'd befriended to her senior prom. He stood us both up on "My Mother's Day from Hell" in 1999. He'd had the habit of making bad choices, but this time he shot himself and his future more than in the foot.

I tried hard to live up to the therapist's prompt to Brad that I seemed to be much more "totally accepting" than his father, that I almost didn't hear him say to my son that this might be a good time for him to tell me something.

"Tell me what?" I'd asked naively.

Then Brad spoke these words: "I guess I'm going to be a dad."

I was speechless, a rare occasion.

"Lily thinks she's pregnant."

"You guess?" I managed to say, bewildered. "Lily thinks? Are you sure?" I mumbled, shaken. I thought he'd broken up with her.

These circumstances were far from the joyous occasion my more grandma-friendly friends had predicted news like this would be. I'd already had six weeks to deal with self-inflicted maternal guilt and parental anger over his getting a DUI, but this? It took me totally by surprise. I had never wanted to hear those words! No sir-eee. I'd been a college health educator for 20-plus years. In spite of the fact his father and I had been divorced since he was four, he'd had all the requisite sit-downs.

"She's sure. She went to the doctor yesterday, after the drugstore pregnancy test said positive."

"*Well yippee*," I screamed inside my head. "*How the fuck could you have done this to me? This is sooooo embarrassing.*

Me. The sex educator. You, the firstborn son to whom I gave The Good Vibrations Kids First Book About Sex *in the fifth grade, and all the free condoms you desired since you were in the sixth. Shit. This goes beyond guilt to shame. How could I have raised a son who could make such a miss-take? GodDAMMIT!"*

But after a deep breath and some quick prayer, out of my mouth came something like, "Well, this is going to take a lot of consideration. Have you two thought of talking to a counselor at Planned Parenthood?"

Abortion as a sound option was the first thing to pop into my 54-year-old feminist women's health professor mind. I couldn't imagine a smiling baby right then; I couldn't even come close to it. This was an accident. A slip-up that needed to be corrected immediately. Lily was a junior in high school, for Christ's sake. Her size-two body that looked so great in tight jeans didn't look like it could lift ten pounds, much less birth a baby. Jesus Christo.

"Neither Lily or I could do that," Brad said, tilting his head with a twisted smile that let me know he was nervous, or knew nothing: *no thing at all*, about the demands of pregnancy and birthing, much less the onerous responsibility to provide that little being with what it needs to grow up and thrive in a less-than-perfect world. For eighteen fucking years … no, for-EVER!

After a long, carefully considered pause I said, "Might we be talking about paternity issues here?"

"You did tell me she saw someone else back then," Mr. Therapist piped up from his leather chair. As he spoke I tried not to notice that he was wearing a toupee, while my son and I simultaneously folded our arms and slouched deeper into opposite ends of a pillowed sofa.

Mea Culpa. What had they gotten us into? Just then I didn't even want to begin to imagine what kind of role either my son or I was going to play in that yet unborn child's life. A grandmother now? Me? Impossible!

To make a long, sordid story short, I angrily left my son at his father's to figure out his own future. When I returned to California,

I immediately crawled on my knees to therapy over my own shame about this. I had planned to tell no one except my current husband and my counselor about the impending birth.

Then, one day in an e-mail to a dear friend and colleague who was a fellow member on a national health list-serve, in a slip of the wrist that could either be called fate or my distracted state at that moment, half the readers of that list-serve got my wailing-wall story. To my amazement, I received several condolence messages, only one of which was filled with horror and judgment. One of the leaders in my field wrote me with empathy. He told me his son had fathered a child five years ago. He had a grandchild he'd never seen and probably wouldn't, ever. The message was implicit: "Get over it, Pat." And the second message was "You're not alone."

To my surprise my therapist suggested I *had* to play some role in that grandchild's life, at least from a distance. She gently pushed me to become the reluctant grandparent I'd so strongly protested before.

My handsome headstrong teenager continued his path of flight, denial, and numbing reality with substances. He ended his "therapy" abruptly, telling the court-appointed shrink, his father and me that he didn't need to talk to anyone, that this was "useless bullshit." He also told both sets of his parents that he was going to "take a year off" before going to college, and he got a job landscaping at a local golf course.

Lily's large extended family embraced her, as many millions in similar places have over the ages. So, at 17, she entered her senior year in high school pregnant, long before it was in movies like *Juno*. By taking no lunch breaks she was able to graduate with honors in January, one month before she was due. I wrote her several letters and received two in return on lined paper in beautifully rounded cursive. In one, dated November 8, 1999, she thanked me for Annie Lamott's *Operating Instructions*, my standard baby gift for *my* friends who had postponed making families until their early 40s, and Penelope Leach's *Your Baby from One to Five*, the bible for post-Spock era feminist moms at the time. In her letter she said,

> "Today I am 26 weeks, the baby loves to move a lot. I have signed up for a Childbirth Preparation Program. There are two classes every week from December 6th to January 10th. I would really like Brad to be my coach. I have only mentioned it to him and have yet to talk to him about it. I will explain to him that I want to look up and see him during labor and delivery. My father told me that at first he didn't really want to go to the birthing classes but now he's glad he did. He said being there watching my sister and I be born was such an incredible experience. I'm so excited!"

I'm glad she couldn't see the look on my face or feel the fear in my heart when I read that. *"How naïve can she be?"* I thought. Writing this now, I just burst into tears as I opened a handmade Christmas card postmarked 15 DEC 1999. A black-and-white photograph of an angel is pasted onto card stock. Written in silver in Lily's script is "Wishing you all the peace and beauty of the Holiday season." Inside are her Class of 2000 high school photo and another letter. In this one, the maturity she gained in the months following her decision to become a mother, with or without my son, amazed me.

> "Thank you for encouraging Brad to come to the classes with me because I very much want him to be a part of this. My mother went with me because Brad says he forgot about the first one. Now he has a new job which he tells me gets him home 8 or 8:30, the time the classes end. I don't want him to be shocked or too surprised by what will happen while I'm in labor. My mother has been very helpful and seems to enjoy herself at the classes.
>   I can relate to you when you say you 'lost sleep' over Brad. I also care about him very much and only want to see him happy. I just wish he'd realize how much I need him. All he seems to care about

sometimes is himself and going out and having a good time. I understand he is a teenage guy, but he needs to become a little bit more responsible and face reality. I have had to change so much in the last seven months. I don't want to sound like I'm complaining because it was my choice to keep this baby and I can't imagine anything ever happening to him or her now, but Brad has made little effort to change his lifestyle."

She was starting to see the writing on the wall. I still have the invitation to Lily's baby shower, its return address from "Nana Laura" dated January 10, 2000. I remember picking out a beautiful white satin nightgown and robe at Macy's for the hospital and sending it to her.

To continue, my firstborn, with my implicit permission (since empty promises can inflict more hurt than the truth), abandoned Lily without making any of her Lamaze classes, and left New York for California. He's seen that beautiful son only once when he was 15 months old, on the day of his younger brother's high school graduation in 2001. And in ten years, I can count on my hands the times I've seen that grandson.

Carter is now 13. Thankfully, his beautiful mom woke up and put her past in the past. Within three years, she married and now has two other beautiful children: a boy now seven and baby girl, three.

In the summer of 2000, when Carter was five months old, with my therapist and partner persistently nudging me to make contact, I visited Lily to see him during a visit to my mother on the east coast. It took three days for me to plow through my resistance and be ready to drive four hours to see my grandson. I met Lily and her striking 46-year-old mother at their home in the rolling farmland where the family-run greenhouse was in full bloom.

Pictures don't lie. There were tears in my eyes in the photo that was snapped when Lily handed me her baby, my grandson. His resemblance to my firstborn made me wince at the accusation of paternity I'd wielded months ago. At first I was afraid I would do something wrong or drop him, feelings I had when I held my own baby for the first time. Then something in his five-month-old smile, his soft skin or the baby smells broke through my reluctance and made me admit I truly was a grandmother. More tears. When the heart opens they flow. Somehow this could be turned into a blessing.

Carter was eighteen months old when my "significant equal" and I decided to get married in Big Sur at what we called our "Seven-Year Hitch." It was the anniversary of the day we'd met and driven there after a spiritual conference at Asilomar on California's central coast. Neither Brad nor his brother Brian, who was in the military, were able to make the trip. We flew Lily, Carter and her husband John out to the wedding in May 2001.

During the outdoor ceremony on a wide lawn overlooking California's most famed view, we gave each of the elders a rose for paving the way for our union, and one to Carter, the youngest in attendance, to pass on the love. This 18-month-old and his beautiful mother stole the show. He sat up quietly through a ceremony that was close to an hour long. Many of the guests complimented Lily on her kind, gentle mothering and her gorgeous child, my grandson. Somewhat, but not completely, I had put aside my reluctance, fear and ego-induced shame. I sent a sigh of gratitude up to the universe, finally realizing how well the spirits had taken care of what I first thought was a terrible mistake.

Distance, time and propriety have kept me in an only partially visible role with this grandson. I kept contact with Lily by e-mail and an occasional phone call. Thanks to the Internet and i-Photo, I've followed the growth of her family. I send special books to Carter every Christmas and birthday. They usually have some positive spiritual twist to them, and are just the kind I'd like to be there to read in person. I'd love to hear him say, "Oh, Grandma, read it a-gain, puh-lease!" But that cannot be. How to sign them continues to be a problem:

Your mystery godmother?

Your surrogate Grandma?

Pat?

Aunt Pat?

Or not sign them at all?

Until recently, I was one among many elders in Carter's lovely extended family, so I usually just settle for Pat, or "California Pat."

Over the years, I have become an annual visitor. I show up on a holiday or summer vacation with a gift or two. Carter avoids addressing me with a family name and just calls me Pat. He's taken me for a walk down the lovely winding rural road he lives on, showing me tadpoles in a stream and naming the vegetation. And this past summer I got to watch a budding personality play games and interact with all sorts of children at the very same lake in which his biological father learned to swim.

As he aged, Carter seemed to resemble Lily's side of the family more than his father's and mine. He has the smooth skin and high cheekbones that Brad did, but darker eyes and hair. At his brother's 5th birthday party that I attended, Lily's sisters and friends from high school remarked to me how much of Brad they saw in Carter, who was being raised in a way totally kinder and slower than I had ever been able to do. He had not spent even one hour with his biological father to explain this imprinting.

That summer I observed Carter make certain movements and heard an expression in his voice that sounded uncannily like his father, my son, at that early age. One day we were playing Ping-Pong. Carter's younger brother and I were a team and he played solo on the other side. He was spot-on good. His shots were carefully placed, his spin hard and direct. (As an adult, his father Brad had won regional dart tournaments in many a bar.) But suddenly, when Carter missed a pivotal shot, he spouted out in anger and threw his paddle at the floor in a way I'd witnessed my impulsive ten-year-old son Brad do decades ago.

And then, even uncannier, I flashed on an ancient memory. When I was nine years old, Jack Wilkin, my father and Carter's biological great granddad, made it to the final round of the 1954

New Jersey Amateur Golf Championships. I was in the gallery. When he missed the putt that lost him the tournament, he took his favorite putter "Goldie" and broke it across his knee! My mother still has the article that ran in the local paper. Weird. I shivered and wondered if an invisible thread could somehow pass on traits like these. Nah. Not so. It was just a coincidence. Right. At that moment, the knot in my stomach prompted me to believe that indeed there was an invisible way character traits can be passed on.

Part Two: Deeper into Invisibility

The second phase of my invisible grandparenting is even more difficult to pull out of my memory banks, but I must. It is about a granddaughter who I haven't seen for the last seven of her eleven years of life. It is sad. It makes me mad. And yet it comes complete with a positive twist that Carter's natural earth mother Lily herself thought of. Both stories have the somewhat happy ending that became the basis for this book and www.invisiblegrandparent. com. Here is how the spirits took care of yet another unintentional (or was it?) pregnancy on my son's part.

Brad continued on what a friend helped me to accept by calling it his hopefully "low road to enlightenment." Some kids wake up from addictions and learn to make better choices before hitting bottom. Others can maintain a life lubricated with whatever makes it feel okay for a long, long time.

Kahlil Gibran's words that were read at my firstborn's christening in 1981 provided some comfort along the way: "Your children come through you, they are not of you. Admittedly they are the arrows that we spring from the bow. We do our best to point it towards center but, as with the wind, much of the outcome is out of our control."

On his 21st birthday, just before I visited Brad and his new girlfriend Suzie in Las Vegas, where they'd moved and both had jobs in Caesar's Palace, Brad said those words again on the phone: "Just so you know, I'm going to be a dad."

I don't remember what my "Yikes!" sounded like this time, but the truth of his "Suzie's six months pregnant," settled in quickly. His east coast father helped me see it with the hope that he would "do it right this time."

Flying to Sin City to hold that precious newborn girl felt a lot different than the first time I held Carter. She was precious. Brad looked happy. They kissed each other good-bye when he went to the store to pick up groceries, even parroting mutual "I love you's" as he left. Suzie looked excited and appeared to be thrilled with motherhood in a way I'd never been. The next Valentine's Day, my son told me he'd gotten on one knee and proposed with a real (small) diamond he'd gotten in a pawn shop.

They decided Vegas was too tough a town in which to raise a child (or keep a job). They left their waiter/server jobs and moved back to California. Happily, I made monthly 350-mile daylong round trips to visit Annie as she progressed from toddler to little girl. We made cookies from scratch, went to the zoo and shopped together for the pink Ariel plastic umbrella she wanted for her 3rd birthday.

Yet sometimes kids can keep a lot hidden from the eyes of in-laws. Suzie didn't complain much, but I detected things were amiss. I watched my son lose jobs, one after another, and his belly grow larger and larger. He went from waiter to busboy, to barbecue smokehouse chef, and finally, took a night shift at a 7-11 convenience store. There always was some reason that he'd been fired or had quit, other than his own inability to tolerate authority, control his anger or limit his consumption of beer.

Then, on one visit, I witnessed a screaming match that in a nano-second would spur any grandmother to grasp her grandchild and run far away with her. Thankfully, I've repressed the details. Suffice it to say that the next day, before Brad came home from wherever he was, Suzie had called her brothers who helped her move out of the apartment.

The depression my son experienced the year following that loss got to him in ways I certainly can understand, but was not very empathetic to back then. Good news: he got a job in construction and was making good money. He also found a new girlfriend, ten years his senior and a surveyor at that. He looked like he was drinking less and had lost some weight. Suzie let him see Annie every other weekend, and asked of me that I make that the only time I see her. Reluctantly, I agreed. I had no choice in the matter.

On most of those visits, the refrigerator in Brad's apartment, which he was sharing with his stepbrother who'd joined him to work in construction, was pretty clean and filled with decent "kid food" like bananas, applesauce and mac and cheese. Brad had become a pretty attentive dad. It showed that he loved his child. I was happy to take them to lunch, the playground, and movies, whatever.

But then things got edgy. Brad broke up with the surveyor. At a Christmas I wasn't able to witness, he showed up with another woman. His brother, my second-born then completing high level military training, called and told me that even he didn't understand this girl, that "something smelled bad." Not literally, of course. She and he were always kind to Annie in front of my ex on their visit from the East, but the girlfriend his brother described for me had the frail frame, bad teeth, slippery eyes and pock-marked face of a meth addict. It took me till late January to get the information out of his stepbrother, that indeed Brad was doing methamphetamine, that it was prevalent in the construction industry in that town.

Needless to say, I flipped out and crawled with humility and horror to my therapist this time. She said I had to do something to protect that child on those weekends my son had been granted "unsupervised" visitation, not without considerable legal struggle.

With Suzie's cooperation, I consulted every rehab and drug addiction specialist from here to New York. I called my ex and told him, but it took three weeks to break through denial that indeed Brad was using meth. Unable to arrange an intervention, as we gained evidence of my son's bad behavior, a letter writing opportunity presented itself that no mother should ever have to face. I had to document to Child Protective Services the reasons my son should not be given visitation rights unless he tested drug free, which he didn't.

February 5, 2007
To: Child Protective Services
From: Pat Hanson, mother of Brad Atherton, grandmother of Annie, Suzie Taylor's daughter

Suzie asked me to write you to document the evidence to back my suspicions that my son Brad has been using methamphetamine, has a history of heavy drinking and marijuana use, and an anger problem that puts unsupervised visitations to my granddaughter Annie at serious risk especially right now. I have a Ph.D. in Health Education from New York University (1981) and a Master's Degree in Applied Behavioral Sciences (1971) from the University of California at Davis. I have read and taught about addictions, mostly from the prevention not treatment point of view; but unfortunately that does not prevent one's own adult children from participating in behaviors that are self-destructive. I have done considerable research on methamphetamine addiction, and know the potential of that erratic drug for unpredicted psychoses.

As you know, between January 20th and February 3rd, we finally informed Suzie of our suspicions about Brad's use of methamphetamine. The rest you know from her documentation. When confronted February 3rd, Brad told my husband and me who drove from Monterey to see him face to face, "Don't darken my door. You'll eat the paperwork for a clean drug test Monday!"

I, his mother, would be glad if that were the case; but I know the research on the extent to which addicts will lie, and use chemicals to test drug free. Indeed, when Brad had to be tested for marijuana, I saw products like Nioxin and other vitamin supplements in his cabinets.

I love my son and want him to get help. I also love

Annie and want her protected. Suzie has questioned Annie and reported to me that Annie told her that "my daddy gives me diamonds … that he makes on the stove …" If that sentence alone from a four-year-old, about actually handling a poisonous illegal substance that he "gave her" isn't enough to prevent unsupervised visitation, for a long long time, I don't know what is. Suzie also told me she has pictures of a burn on Annie's arm that happened sometime last fall, Brad says "by accident." And Suzie also said Annie mentioned a "fire" at a trailer in the woods.

Thank you for your professional assistance in this case. Please feel free to contact me directly for any further information.

Not easily, I have put the memory of those few horrid months years ago far behind me. In retrospect, remembering my minister's admonition "there are two sides of every story and then the truth," I wonder if Suzie didn't exaggerate some of the details she reported to me. They sound so typical of the movies or an Internet search that a spurned mother with an active imagination might make up. Later she told me she'd lost the pictures of the burn.

I'm happy to report that my son has moved beyond the addiction and bad choices that marked that period in his life. But at that time, in spite of great protest and accusations that I, his "psycho mom," would eat my words. Brad failed the drug test twice. He blew up at me, as did his father who, needing to have someone to blame, shouted, "How come you never supported your son?" After that, even after hiring a private investigator, neither his father nor I heard from him for a harrowing 18 months. Once he did reach out to his military brother, who drove 400 miles to visit him at a favorite fishing spot in the hills.

"Brad looked good," he told us. He'd denied he was using, but did sign a contract his brother made him write, that he would never borrow money from his father again and he'd stay in contact. Neither happened. Much to the entire family's chagrin, he didn't even make it to his brother's graduation from one of the most prestigious military training programs in the United States. I took it as a sign of hope that ten minutes to midnight on Mother's Day during that period, he called. "Mom, it's me Brad," he went on as I almost fainted, my heart was beating so loudly.

"Don't ask me any questions, or I'll hang up," he said, "I just wanted to say Happy Mother's Day." I told him how glad I was to hear his voice, that I always loved him and always would. End of conversation.

The following Christmas I heard from his brother that Brad had found a new girlfriend who encouraged him to reach out to his family. He started with a cousin, and then she encouraged him to call his father. Somehow my son had escaped early enough from the downward spiral that accompanies meth addiction. My ex and his wife Julie visited him and said he looked fine.

He never contacted me directly. It took another nine months, but on Thanksgiving Day of 2008, when I opened the door of my in-laws' house, there with my soldier son who we'd expected, stood Brad! It had been almost two years since I'd seen him.

"I'd have called you Mom, but I wanted to surprise you and see if you'd have a heart attack!"

Before I could give him the proverbial slap-across-the-side-of-his-head that he deserved, he gave his mom a big bear hug. My tears made a visible imprint on his pressed white shirt.

He doesn't call me often. But he has on the Mother's Days since, always late in the day near midnight. I only have a P.O. box for him, not an address. As far as I know, he's living in the Sierras working two jobs, one for a ski patrol and the other cutting trees. This year he didn't call on my birthday. But hey, I've stopped obsessing about his life. It's his journey that I couldn't have predicted and certainly can't control. It's his road to walk, and whether that is to enlightenment or mediocrity is not up to me.

For five months, back when their separation started, Suzie allowed me to drive over monthly and have daylong visits with Annie. Happily ensconced in a new relationship, she'd actually had a newborn little sister for Annie and was planning her own wedding. Then, one day, she stopped answering my calls. For weeks that became months she would not return messages. Sometimes I curse caller ID.

I asked my ex and Julie for her address, as I'd heard they had gotten to visit when they were across country. But they told me she specifically had asked them not to give it to her. Julie even sneaked in a Christmas present from me to their collection of mailed packages; but I didn't dare fully identify myself. It was a stuffed penguin, and a copy of a new DVD on penguins. I was hoping it might remind her it was I who'd given her *Happy Feet* and watched it with her over and over. That would have to do.

I slid deeper into invisibility and depression. I couldn't understand why I was specifically being asked not to be a presence at all in the life of a young girl who I had seen almost monthly until she was four. I figured that her mom was, and still is, choosing to erase every memory that she can of her real father out of her daughter's mind. Unfortunately, that included me, who she must consider to be an aging hippie grandma.

But is that possible, at four? What I understood even less is that she asked my ex and his wife, who play grandpa and grandma on annual visits to California, not to give me her number or address. Angry at first, it appeared to me that they colluded with Suzie's request to keep me out of the picture. Then I understood that of course they would! They wouldn't want to jeopardize their ability to see her the one time a year they make it from the East to the West Coast.

With more than a little exasperation, I ran to several more therapy sessions to swallow yet another test of my sanity. I pondered what I might have done to deserve such treatment. The old "Why me?" and even the "Why not them?" reared its ugly head. *They* get to remain visible. Huh? Let me spare you my thoughts at the time on that one.

My therapist, who I still needed for sure, told me personally she knew of three cases similar to mine. She suggested that at some point in the future my granddaughter might look me up. That didn't help. All I hoped then was that by that time I'd not be too old, and of sound enough body and mind to communicate all the love that I had been bottling up all this time.

I knew there were others out there like me. Surely other invisible grandparents had fantasies that someday a grown woman or man will knock on their door, or seek them out for a reunion on a television talk show. But at that time I didn't know where to turn for solace and comfort.

Part Three: Writing Letters Helps Heal Hurt

I used to exclaim, "Out of the mouths of babes," but now I say, "Out of the mouths of babes who have become mothers!" Writing letters to the grandchildren to whom I am invisible has helped me reconcile and heal the circumstances surrounding my situation. And it was all Lily's idea. I may be invisible, but I can still have a voice.

During the period Brad was missing, I had confided in Lily, who by then had married and had given Carter a brother. I told her that Brad had a drug problem and was nowhere to be found. She'd heard about Suzie and Annie years before.

Lily, lovely mother of two at all of 23, had a great idea! She called me with the news that Carter was developing a yet-to-be-defined writing/reading disability. He was being encouraged in school to write letters. She asked me for the address of his half-sister. I told her sadly that I didn't have it, and hadn't been able to make contact with Annie for 18 months.

I told her I had not heard from Brad in that time, despite the fact that my ex-husband and his wife, the other set of biological grandparents, had her address and have even seen her. Back then, after hearing my story with understandable empathy, beautiful mother Lily said, "Why don't you write Annie letters and save them?"

Boink! Lightbulbs went off in my head!

What … a … great … idea!

She suggested I write letters to her, bundle them and save them for that day my therapist said might happen. How my heart was touched! As I wrote the first letter, an incredible weight seemed to lift off my shoulders. Some unintentional healing was beginning. I found the process incredibly therapeutic. I kept writing letters. Slowly but surely I realized that process was helping me get over past hurts. In the prologue you witnessed my first letter to Annie on her first day of school.

Since then I've written dozens of letters and discovered that there are lots of others out there like me. By speaking out about my "identity" at a national conference I discovered I was one of an undetermined number of adults whose grown children, for some reason, have kept their identity, as well as their participation out of the lives of their children. Invisibility hurts, especially around the holidays. But writing letters and saving some, while purposely releasing others in order to move toward forgiveness, helps.

With the grace of God/Goddess/higher power, whatever you call it, I have come to surrender and not fight this situation. I'm working on forgiveness. Forgiveness of my own son, forgiveness for the mother who has banished me from the life and mind of my granddaughter, and last but not least, forgiveness of myself. I had raised my two sons in a nontraditional long-distance joint custody arrangement, and in weak moments somehow I thought I was being punished for the way I'd parented and it was coming back to haunt me.

In *My Legacy of Letters* you will see many of my letters were about places I'd been that were special to my sons. Some contained fond memories. Others were wistful values-laden letters about the high costs of war and the presidential election. Many contained advice on things like "thank-you notes are important" and "my broken listener." Some were about aging, others about death and letting go, like when a hospice client of mine had died. One day I found myself addressing topics and talking in a voice more appropriate for a young adult or teen-age listener.

Sometimes as I folded a letter and put it in the special chest I'd found for it, something special happened that made me more at peace with the situation. I found myself intending the best for Annie, and actually visualizing it, in the form of affirmative prayer.

However, other days I couldn't suppress the resentment, the anger that this was happening to me. I was angry that I couldn't transmit my values and model aging gracefully, directly. Invisiblity hurt. My first reaction was to get angry and self-righteous and scream about all the good things my grandchildren will miss out on, me at the top of the list. So I decided to intentionally write a few letters that I told myself I would never save. I did not want my grandchild, or anyone for that matter, to feel the negative energy in them.

I developed two categories of letters: those to be "Save and Share Someday" (SSS) and those to "Said but Never Send" (SNS). As a writer, I couldn't help but save a copy of a few of my angry letters. Here is my first SNS letter:

Christmas Hurts!
December 18, 2008
Dear Annie,

I was just bending over the kitchen sink, crying. Sobbing. I don't want to turn on the radio and listen to cheery Christmas music, or go into stores and watch everybody spending money on the gifts and the special foods they make every year. This year, the thought of opening the beautiful decorations I store in a box for eleven months and looking forward to hearing you say how much you like the bubble lights, gives me a stomach-ache. I want to watch you see everyone exclaiming, "Oooh! The surfer girl! Grandpa gave me that one when I was in college," or hear you say, "The crystal icicles are my favorite," or me say, "I remember when Grandma gave me this one of the graduate in cap and gown when I got my Ph.D!"

All of this makes me very very sad. And mad.
I was sad, really sad this morning, reading the

newspaper today. I wanted to buy tickets for you for the dance performance of "The Velveteen Rabbit," instead of "The Nutcracker" this year. "Thank you, Grandma," I can hear you say. "I loved the sugar plum fairy and all the ballerinas last year, but that show was soooo long!"

I want to be buying a tiny tree you could string popcorn for, and to have you help me cook the turkey dinner. It's your voice I want to hear asking me to make a favorite recipe of mine, like the pink molded cranberry salad Uncle Ted loved and always helped whip the cream for.

But most of all, I was crying because your mother (I want to curse her soul at the moment, but even in this "to be said and not sent" letter, I find myself unable to be too "mean.") But your f---ing mother (there, that felt good! At least I got out a nasty word) had the audacity (meaning the balls! the not-good sense), to send me her "Atherton Family Sending You Holiday Hugs Card" with no return address on it! All that was inside the envelope was a picture of the five of you. Five, wow! I see you have a new baby brother or sister. Maybe that's all your mom wanted to tell me, to show me, but Jesus! What a way to do it!

Suzie doesn't have a clue what it feels like to be blocked from having the kind of family that actually makes contact with one another, especially at holidays!

Forgive me, God, but that woman in all her hormonal breastfeeding miasma must have a really twisted and distorted sense of herself and me to do this! They say what goes around comes around, but I write this in hopes that you, my little Annie, have the good sense never to do this to the mother of your children's children. I don't want you to even imagine what it would feel like if, someday, someone took your own grandchildren, Suzie's great-grandchildren, away. Far far away, leaving no address or way to contact them. Asking the other grandparents who do get to see you once a year when they're in *from the East coast, not to give me your address! And then to send a picture at Christmas time! A picture is supposed to equal a thousand words. Hmmm, I wonder what sentences would come out after all this silence and distance! I doubt they would be pretty.*

I have some ideas of why she is now keeping you from seeing me, even after, in truth, it was I who was protecting you by turning your biological father into Child Protective Services for using drugs that could endanger your safety on unsupervised visits; but I'll save that for another letter.

I'd sure like to tell Julie and Sam, your biological father's parents, my version of the truth about your mom. They are the grandparents you do see sometimes, who I'm sure have already sent you a bunch of cool presents to be opened under the tree. But I am going to spare you the negative energy by writing these words, but then burning them. Really. I will be putting them in a bowl outside and setting the paper on fire, watching the words disintegrate and turn into ash and blow away. To be forgotten, I wish!

Merry Christmas. Take a look at this picture of the way Larry and I put the lights on our houseplants. With no children around we've stopped decorating a tree.

F---! S---! P--s! This hurts!

Please, Annie , may you grow up with the good sense to communicate the truth clearly to everyone you deal with, and not get caught up in a bunch of distorted lies.

Christmases hurt for me. May yours be memorably merry!

I love you!

Your invisible grandma.

PAT

P.S. Bah. Humbug! Enough of this. Being grateful for where I am right now and what I do have helped me to

forget what I don't. I'm going to drive to the gym in the
65-degree sunshine this 18th of December, and work out
to some rock-n-roll. Then swim outdoors in the heated
pool.
  I will not wallow in this.
  I will not wallow in this.

Over the past four years I continued writing these phantom letters at least once a month, and will keep it up until … until … until? I believe that if other parents and grandparents burdened with invisibility wrote their own letters, a movement of positive intention for future generations could emerge. We grandparents, kept in the shadows, can have a voice at least, even if we can't be "seen." By writing, we too can have an opportunity to express our own feelings about our virtual entrapment.

By forgiving others and ourselves, we set ourselves free. If more of us engage in rituals for expressing negative feelings honestly, followed by a safe way to collectively let go of negative vibrations, while "holding the high watch for that child," who knows what good may follow? Setting an intention of forgiveness, toward the people, places and things that resulted in our situation, can lift a huge burden from our shoulders. Forgiving ourselves is equally important. It may actually free us to pass on to younger generations the memories and values we feel important.

Today, instead of pouting and listing what was missing from my life that I have no control over, I'm putting a different vibration out there. It encourages and articulates our love for those little ones. It promotes forgiveness. Please join me in my journey. Many of us are facing similar non-traditional family hurdles. Perhaps we can help each other, and still make a difference in the lives of the yet-to-be. Leave a legacy of love whether you can be there or not.

Update Twelve Years Later—Heart-full-ness!

September 12, 2012

My heart is full. Yesterday I sat in a beach chair in sunny Santa Barbara, California, and one of my boys (now 29) asked me to rub sunscreen on his military muscular triangular back. His older brother (now 31) was already out beyond the breakers standing on a paddleboard. What a reunion! Where had the twenty+ years gone since the annual summer trips we took to Aunt Jean's house blocks from the beach? Then I had applied the same sunscreen to six-and eight-year old backs. Boogie boards were their favorite way to ride the waves. Later skateboards became the chosen way to ride the streets to the wharf for ice cream, and buy star-shaped wands to dip in huge vats of bubbles.

My heart is bursting because there were years at a time, not long ago, that I hadn't heard from my oldest child and didn't even know where he was. There were also many months when, heart in my throat, I couldn't hear from his younger brother because he was in Iraq or Afghanistan or Bahrain.

My heart also tugs as I finally write this, because of those missing from this family reunion. Annie will be ten in October and my only contact with her has been in my dreams. My heart is wide open, because a year ago I traveled 3,000 miles and saw my now 12-year-old grandson, who now has specifically been told by his wonderful mother and step-dad that "Pat from California" who rolls by once a year, is his biological grandmother. I hadn't realized they'd told Carter long ago that he was adopted, that his dad "just wasn't ready to settle down" long ago. Here is a recent letter from Lily to me after reading the text for this entire manuscript. This time it is not in cursive, but via computer:

> "It's a little embarrassing reading these letters I wrote. It's hard for me to remember that girl I was. We have never withheld the facts about John adopting Carter when he was two. I have always told him that you are his biological grandmother. It wasn't like we sat down with him one day

and surprised him with this news. I thought and still think the best way to handle it is have it all be out in the open. I will and have always answered any of Carter's questions honestly. He just hasn't asked many.

When we did have a discussion about Brad (probably about a year ago now) I asked Carter if he could imagine our 17-year-old neighbor (who he knows well) as a father. He said "no way!" I think he somewhat understood why Brad moved to California. I couldn't understand then, but know now that him moving to California was the best thing he could have done for me. I honestly couldn't be happier with my life now, Pat. John has given me everything I have ever dreamed of."

Lily—October 11, 2012

It's also been almost four years since I had the inclination to write a book about *Invisible Grandparenting* that would address my own pain, and my own not fully finished path to rising above circumstances out of my control to heal the separation I feel from two grandchildren. In these years I've learned that we all can be able to leave a legacy of something, anything, especially of love, to our own grandkids or any children for that matter.

It's been two years since I developed and started blogging at my website www.invisiblegrandparenting.com, attracting comments from others who identify with my situation. It's been a full three months, home in a foggy Monterey summer (winter) that I've had the time, nothing on my teaching or speaking schedule, to write.

At first I fell into what I called a depression, avoiding telling this story of my own long-distance parenting. For a while, I internalized the blame and shame directed at me by some family members and friends way back when, and I found myself thinking this situation was "my fault." I couldn't rise above guilt, the gift that keeps on giving, even with the very healing exercises I had used in workshops I'd run with other invisible grannies and aunties you will see in the next chapters.

But now, witness these pages, I've finally found the courage and the energy to pull the volumes of material I've written on

Invisible Grandparenting into form and fruition. I am now geared up to not only bare my own soul, but to encourage others to do so in a way that can help us rise above our "stories," attempt to let go of bitterness, and leave a legacy for the children who will outlive and outlast us.

HANDLING INVISIBILITY

"Mother's Day is the Most Difficult Day of the Year" was the header to this blog I wrote on May 13, 2012, on my website.

> Dear Invisible Grandparents of all kinds:
> You are all especially on my mind today. Each of you in one way or another has contributed to more of us feeling less alone with our "stories." Thank you.
> *"Mothers hold their children's hands for a little while, but they hold their hearts forever"* was the quote on the program in my church this morning. When the children came in to sit in front of the choir, I got misty-eyed as I do every week. I told myself to forget about wondering what my granddaughter looked like now at almost ten, or whether she was getting any spiritual upbringing at all.
> I just wondered, hoped and *knew* in my heart that all grandmothers hold the love for their kids and grandkids involuntarily deep in their hearts. Only we Invisible Grandparents are challenged to do it to even greater levels!
> My blessings to all of us out there, invisible or not. May we all fill our waking moments with as much love, positivity and wonderful experiences as possible.

How We Cope

I interviewed dozens of invisible grandparents from all over the United States. Their situations and solutions varied widely but in each, time was a common theme that helped them heal, or at the least accept, their circumstances and surrender to "what is, is." As each moved toward recovering emotionally or spiritually, they found paths to moving on with their own lives. Many of them turned to prayer, and found ways to "hold the high watch" for their grandchildren, imagining their lives turning out successfully.

There are countless ways each of us challenged with separation deal with our anxiety, our pain, and our particular sense of the situation. Many of the "defense mechanisms" we find ourselves engaged in would not be considered "healthy" by experts, but hey, they just are. We do or did what we needed to do. Some of us may have found more gracious ways to cope, to heal for a while and try to keep "out of sight, out of mind." Others chose to take legal steps regarding visitation. For most, however, the process of dealing with the grief of invisible grandparenting is a series of cycles: a few steps forward, and then a few back, then more toward serenity.

At first many of us found ourselves wondering what in the world we could have done to deserve this. We may deny the strength of our feelings, or find ways to block, suppress or numb them. Alcohol, shopping, work and distractions of all kinds, some addictive, may help us forget for a while. We may become depressed, turning bitterness and anger inward, blaming and shaming ourselves. We may withdraw and isolate, wishing our secret pain would go away.

Acting out with expressions of anger directed at those adults we perceive as responsible can and does occur, and may even involve acts bordering on stalking. Badmouthing, blaming and shaming the parents, resenting their very being may also occur.

Yet others of us may find healthier, more gracious ways to understand and live with our situation. Sharing your story with a close friend, a therapist or a clergyman may help you "feel the feelings," and eventually realize that "the only way out is through." Letting yourself experience the tears, the grief, and even the resentments, can help you *not* put the vibration of negative energy of anger out to affect anyone, especially ourselves. Participating in support groups or on-line discussions may help.

Some of those I interviewed chose to become substitute or surrogate grandparents. They offered their skills as "grandma for hire" to close friends or relatives, offering to travel with other's children, or have them visit their homes. Thousands of young adults need positive role models in their lives. The Appendix contains contact information for national programs available in your community on "foster grandparenting," or mentoring and literacy programs that need volunteers.

What follows are stories from the actual steps invisible grandparents took to handle separation and rise above circumstances beyond their control. The names and locations in all stories have been changed.

The Interviews

Darrie: Early Memories from Therapy Lead to Accusations

Darrie, now 59, remarried at 50, six years after the father of her three children—two sons and a daughter died. Two of her sons live in Japan. She has kept a long-distance relationship with those grandchildren by writing letters and sending packages. She even Skypes them at Christmas and watches them open their presents.

However, it is her relationship with her daughter and a 10-year-old granddaughter that lives nearby that has led her to see three therapists, "but I don't think I've found the right one yet," Darrie told me. Seven years ago her 32-year-old daughter in her own therapy uncovered a memory that she had been molested as a child for a full year, twice a week, not by a family member, but by a babysitter's teenage son. She became angry with her mother for not knowing this and somehow "fixing" the situation. Darrie's daughter thinks her mother is "not safe now" to babysit or even see her children, in spite of the fact that they live only 60 miles away, and Darrie helped out and was there every week the first eight months of the baby's life. "She's stopped talking with me and is even trying to pollute Darrie's relationship with her brothers in Japan," she reported.

In addition to seeking professional counseling, this is how Darrie coped with her grief. "At first, I couldn't think of that baby girl's name without sobbing, so I visited on-line websites and classrooms where I chatted with other parents and grandparents in similar situations. She also prays for her granddaughter and visualizes her surrounded in a golden bubble. Darrie consciously imagines good things happening in her life.

Darrie would love to do all the day-to-day grandparenting of this granddaughter, i.e., taking her on vacations, seeing her skills grow as she learns to swim in a nearby lake, and watching her participate in school sports. Instead in order to leave a legacy, she's started a scrapbook of "Tidbits," listing things she'd want her granddaughter to know. With pictures and mementos Darrie writes down "how I think about things right now," and as she ages, "I'll change these notes as I imagine how I'd interact with her if I were able to be present."

Shawna: Addictions and the Courts
Complicate the Situation

When her two children were teenagers, they told Shawna now 63, they never wanted children so she thought the traditional grandparenting she'd heard so much about would never happen to her. However at 19, her daughter Iris, then a cake decorator at Safeway, got pregnant. Shawna became frightened since Iris was so young, and she'd heard reports that her daughter's boyfriend had been into hard drugs.

As the truth of her daughter's situation unraveled, Shawna learned that Iris didn't do any drugs herself until the baby was 18 months old, and her now ex-boyfriend had gotten involved with another woman. Anxious about mothering 24/7, and in pain from the break-up, that boyfriend gave the mother of his child the ultimate pain reliever: heroin. Reports about Iris that the baby was often left unattended circulated among neighbors and got back to Shawna. Shawna actually took her grandson from the household, and for the next 16 years co-parented him every other week with his father's parents, who now have him full time.

That not being enough to handle, Shawna is also the invisible grandparent of four other children, only one of whom she sees on a limited basis 500 miles from her home.

Iris got into her first rehab and survived eight months clean, but then met an older Mexican man, Jóse, who although he already had a family of three grown children, wanted a son. Iris and Jóse lived with his mother and assorted relatives, and she conceived Theresa while using hard drugs.

Shawna accepted this situation as well as she could. She gave her daughter a shower with friends from her hometown. After the baby was born an eight-hour drive away, Shawna found a friend in Social Services where her daughter lived, who reported to her the details of what was going on with her grandchild.

Long, painfully sad story short: Theresa was developmentally delayed at birth. The baby had neurological issues, learning disabilities, and physical handicaps all due to prenatal drug use by Iris. The hospital and Social Services kept the baby. Luckily she was placed with a foster family who nursed her to health and wanted to adopt her.

Subsequently Iris moved back in with Jóse and had two other babies, both girls. Reports kept circulating to Social Services that Iris's children were wandering around outside the home neglected, one time having gotten out through a cat door. Theresa had been taken away and given back to Iris not once but eleven times by the courts, within a four–year period. Each time she'd show up in court cleaned up on methadone, and make an appeal to the judge. Theresa's original foster parents eventually gave up and found another child to adopt. Her two sisters were placed in a foster home together.

At one point a judge was going to remove all three girls from their foster homes because he thought they all should be placed in one home together. Social Services attempted to find one home but was unsuccessful. Frustrated with the system, and concerned that the judge might award her grandchildren back to her daughter who was reported to be drinking heavily, Shawna wrote a letter to the judge in hopes he would never move the children again. She still held out hope that Iris would rehabilitate and be reunified with her daughters. Shawna accompanied her plea for continuity to the judge with letters from three relatives who'd observed Iris's behavior over the years. Stating the need for stability, she recommended her grandchildren stay with and be adopted by their foster parents.

As a result of these letters Iris was placed in a residential rehab program that worked to reunify mothers with their children. There was one stipulation, however: Iris was not to see or contact Jóse. Iris lasted only two weeks, probably because the detox from methadone was too difficult. Jóse came and got her and she left. Soon after, Iris finally delivered the boy that the father had wanted all these years.

Theresa's first foster parents, who had raised her from infancy had given up hope and found another baby. She was adopted by a lesbian couple, her second set of foster parents, and who now welcome Shawna's long-distance contacts and visits saying, "She knows you, she remembers you, you're the only consistent memory in her life." The next two girls have been adopted together by a family who is very protective and does not allow any contact with the grandmother. The boy is being cared for and now legally adopted by a relative of Jóse's.

So how does this quadruple invisible grandparent cope?

"In a sense it'd be easier to not be involved because it was so sad. I was totally in love with my first grandson since he was born. I knew I had to play a role in the others so that they could be in a safe, stable environment, but it's been a challenge. As much as I can, I try not to let it devastate me. I refuse to let it take me down. My yoga helps; I probably would've killed myself really. I couldn't have borne the pain my daughter numbs herself not to feel from having her kids taken away. I was in therapy years ago and what I learned there helps me now.

"When I start to worry, I picture God holding each of these little ones, like Santa Claus, in his lap. In the big picture somehow that's what really is. I've been as helpful as I could, but I learned you have no control over anybody. You can lead them to the resurrection, but ultimately they have to choose their own life.

"Today the two little girls are with a teacher who's afraid to let them know me and wants no contact. I can't send presents even through the social service agency. I'm hoping someday maybe she'll allow it, but I'm not holding my breath. They are my grandchildren, but there are all types of ways people grandparent. However the adoptive parents of these kids want to be with me, I have to accept that.

"What one thing would I say to other invisible grandparents? 'What is is, try to make the best of it. It's a struggle sometimes, but I accept what is. My daughter is a drug addict and alcoholic, and now at 35 the chances of her getting it together are slim. When I was faced with reports about Iris nodding out or asleep—and this had been going on for 4½ years—I realized the odds of her getting clean and sober after at least four rehabs and even jail were slim. I had to search my soul before I wrote that letter to the courts, but after so many false attempts I did it. My sense for those little ones was to urge the courts that they have some sense of permanence in their lives. Now Theresa's adoptive moms say, 'You're the only person she knows, she remembers you.' Perhaps when the other kids get older they'll want to know their grandmother better, but I can't spend my days hoping for that.

"I've been blessed recently with my husband who is a wonderful sensitive man and knew about my kids and their history. That could've scared many men away. It's lonely out there; now I have someone to grow old with, a companion. I'm thankful for everything I do have."

Alia: A Metaphysical Perspective

Alia, 69, was divorced at 30 from her first husband of 13 years, a philanderer. She remarried her present husband of 30 years when her a son was 13 (now 46) and her daughter 10 (now 43). She has two grandchildren (Alex, 13, and Victoria, 10) by her son. He had taken over his biological father's trucking business after his dad died at 60 in 1998. Alia had a parting of ways with her son and daughter-in-law over the family business that failed and went bankrupt five years ago. In spite of apologizing in every way possible—in person, by phone, in writing and even text messages—Alia and her son, and of course the grandchildren, have not spoken since then, almost fourteen years. Packages that she sends on holidays and birthdays get returned "UNCLAIMED" in the mail.

A lifelong spiritual seeker and member of Unity churches, Alia pursued some very creative practices, to deal with and heal from her situation. Looking back, she realized how much time and internal work it took to heal from her first divorce.

"I remember standing in a shower back then, feeling that all the water pouring over me was my own tears. At some point I realized the hate I felt towards this 'other woman' was only hurting me. So I said The Lord's Prayer."

For a year, every time she felt negative, she repeated The Lord's Prayer in her head. "It took me fully five years to get over the hate, grief and pain I felt, but I did."

As a metaphysical seeker Alia said, "I don't want to perpetuate the vibration of anger and fear. I know it won't do any good. If I can release my anger, forgive my son and daughter-in-law, that's important. I believe my karmic path is about love, and that I have been confronted with these issues of being misunderstood and betrayal for a reason: to clean them up."

One day Alia found a piece of jewelry: a gold heart with a loop on top that her daughter had given her grandmother, who passed away five years ago. That same day she came across a heart-shaped bar of soap on a rope with "I love you grandma" on it. She hung both in her bathroom.

"Every time I wash my hands I say, 'I love you too,' thinking of Alex and Victoria the grandkids I haven't seen in five years. There's also a poem on a plaque I bought years ago. I thought I'd put it on the wall, but to date I've not been able to. While I've come a long way, this process of healing is never ending," Alia said.

Alia's mom, in her 80's, once asked Alia what it was like to really forgive someone, as well as one's self. "I could kick myself," was one of her mother's favorite expressions. "Well," she told me,

"I decided right then and told my mother, 'my goal at the moment of my death, is to be satisfied with my life. Not rich, not famous, just satisfied'." It appears Alia has already made it quite far on that path.

In October 2012, Alia e-mailed me this note to update her status:

> Honey—I haven't been able to find that poem. So sorry. Nothing has changed between me and my son and family. Last December I went back to Illinois to see my grandson dance the leading role in the "Nutcracker Suite," he was then 14. I saw them all. Michele my daughter-in-law made eye contact with me once or twice.
>
> Everyone was cordial but after I came back home it was exactly the same. Not even a Christmas photo card. I am struck by profound sadness as I write this, but mostly I have turned it all over to the Universe. I have a full life—to say the least—and I love my life. I don't know what is in the future for me and my first-born son—when I pray I pray to Divine Mother—who "knows" my heartache. But for the most part my life goes on "oooblah dee, oooblah dah."

Roxanne: A Therapist's Personal Challenge

As a single mom in her late 40s, Roxanne, a Ph.D therapist, adopted a three-year-old daughter, June, who she soon discovered had "attachment disorder." A person with attachment disorder has problematic social relationships and behaviors from an early age that might involve excessive friendliness and inappropriate approaches to strangers. It can result from unusual early experiences of neglect, abuse or frequent change of caregivers before age three. When youngsters with this disorder become parents, they are unable to respond to cues required for the healthy emotional development of their children.

After a troublesome adolescence and periods of living on the street, as well as stretches of therapy and medications, which unfortunately never lasted, Roxanne's daughter had five children with five different fathers between the ages of 19 and 37. At 40 she discovered she had cervical cancer. She died five years later.

At nineteen, after one abortion, Roxanne and June brought her first baby home. Within one month, although Roxanne bonded with that grandbaby, they agreed that June was not ready for motherhood, and went through an open adoption process. They both agreed on the baby's adoptive parents and had to let go of feelings of separation surrounding that child. Three years later June's friends talked her into trying to get the baby back. For another three years, there was a series of, in Roxanne's own words, "clueless social workers and horrible court trials," while the adoptive parents fought for her.

With June living on the streets, Roxanne unsuccessfully stood against her own daughter in court, but the public defender believed June, who had carefully orchestrated the trial, charmed and conned him. The judge had not taken time to question the stable grandmother.

Roxanne reports, "At first I was helping June be a good mom. Then I was forced to try to keep my first grandchild from being on the street with my daughter. I wanted to protect this child!"

After a long period of estrangement from her mother, June moved two-thirds of the way across the country and had a third child Tyler with Ralph, whom she married, and settled in to operate as a family. For several years Roxanne visited twice a year. Although the trailer they lived in was what she called a "disaster," she would sit down and play games with Tyler, and he sees her as his grandma.

To this day other relatives in that state thank Roxanne for her presence in Tyler's life. She maintained a consistent presence in Tyler's life by paying for pre-school, sending toys and games, and calling several times a month during the five years that his mother's health declined because of cervical cancer. Though she disapproved of the way her daughter parented, "He was raised on Mountain Dew and junk food, but her grandchild had bonded with his father and loved school." Roxanne was the grounded presence that took Tyler under her wing when his mother died, the day after he graduated from kindergarten.

A few years later another chapter of separation began again. Tyler's dad married a woman this therapist saw as truly disturbed. They stopped taking calls from Roxanne and returned mail she sent on holidays. Tyler's communication with Roxanne dwindled and he seemed powerless to her.

As a result Roxanne researched grandparent's rights, and took the family to court. She was allowed weekly phone calls, and to send presents, but needed to have everything monitored by Ralph. Tyler, who for close to ten years could speak freely to his grandmother, now could not speak to her alone, and had to have calls by speakerphone. Roxanne told me that Tyler said under his breath, "This is atrocious." Roxanne for now has settled into twice-yearly visits and weekly phone calls, albeit monitored, but sees this as a terrible strain on Tyler. "But, it's better than nothing," she claims.

In the interim Roxanne has found out about her other grandchildren. June's firstborn is in veterinary school, the second who was raised by his grandparents is doing well three states away.

Concerning her feelings around all this, Roxanne reports, "Over the last two years I've felt so gray inside, there was so much pain around it, it was like a second death. I don't think I handled it. You just live with it. It's awful. This kid was my only connection to my daughter who is now dead. I've talked to him twice a week on the phone ever since he could barely talk. It was a sudden, terrible loss. I couldn't speak to him, and didn't know if he got the presents I sent. So I sent a few books through his school, cause I wanted to make sure he'd get them. They brought that up in court, and I was very calm about it.

"It's just very painful. I think by going to court, Tyler knows how hard I've tried to see him. I don't know what I'd have done if they blocked me completely. Separation is the greatest pain in the world. I don't know quite how I would've coped, quite honestly. You feel so helpless, and so wronged. Though I have a very good life, I think I was struggling with minor depression. To have the father that I've supported and helped out suddenly just cross me out of his life—it's just awful. The word *invisible* just doesn't work for me. It's not strong enough. You're not grandparenting, you're cut off. I'm his grandmother and I don't get to see him, I'm cut off."

What's actually helped Roxanne is her connections to other members of the family. "There's an aunt back there who says to me, 'We miss him so much and can't see him either, but we're so glad you can.' What selfless beautiful people they are!"

What words of wisdom would this professional counselor like to pass on to other invisible grandparents? "People need to talk to others and get in community with other men and women who've experienced the same thing. Your website could make a difference in lots of lives. Do what you can to heal, and know you'll be living with the loss. Erich Fromm said separation is the cause of all anxiety. Do what you can, but get on with your own life. Live with the loss. You're not a victim. Life handed you a crummy deal, now you're you gonna handle it."

Gloria: From Pain to Advocacy

Gloria, 64, retired from a counselor's position with the Department of Education after 22 years. She was married and had her daughter Diana in 1976. Gloria raised her daughter alone from the time she was 11 months old. Diana grew to become a bright, independent young woman. She married at 24 in 2000 and gave birth to three children. Whenever Gloria babysat, her grandchildren were always excited to learn that she would be staying overnight. Her daughter was thankful that her mother took such good care of her babies.

Gloria celebrated most holidays and birthdays with her daughter, son-in-law, and grandchildren. She attended every concert, holiday show and all of her grandchildren's activities. Gloria did not hesitate to assist her daughter whenever she was needed.

Yet, there were many times when Gloria was hurt by her daughter's rude and unexplainable behavior toward her. Her daughter lied many times about the facts to justify her cruel behavior toward her mother. Gloria suspected that the couple's mission was to alienate her from the children for unjust reasons, so she was cautious not to overstep her boundaries as a parent and grandparent. As time went on, she rarely felt comfortable in their home.

In 2004, Gloria told her daughter and son-in-law that she could not understand why they treated her as they did and suggested they seek counseling together. In a therapy session, Gloria described her daughter and son-in-law's behavior towards her as cruel and bizarre. When the therapist questioned the couple about their behavior toward Gloria, her son-in-law admitted that they had been "a little harsh."

Eventually, Gloria became separated and then estranged from her grandchildren. In 2008, Gloria's daughter excluded her mother from her usual Christmas Eve sleepover. Instead she invited her father and her in-laws for dinner. It was the first Christmas Eve ever that Gloria was excluded from celebrating with her family.

For months after that, Gloria's telephone calls and emails to her daughter and son-in-law requesting visits were ignored. Gloria began experiencing symptoms of depression and sought counseling. Her doctor prescribed an antidepressant to help her cope with the emotional pain she felt due to the difficult times with her daughter.

After her daughter's blocking her mother for five months, and numerous attempts to resolve any issues that existed, Gloria filed an application for mediation in the Family Court of the state where her grandchildren resided. She appeared with proof of a history of the relationship with both parents and an established, trusting relationship with her three grandchildren from the time they were born. Her records included all the dates she babysat, invited sleep-overs, shared holidays and birthdays.

Her daughter and her husband chose to hire an attorney, however. They then decided not to show up for the mediation. After the date of mediation, the court summoned both parties to appear before a judge. Gloria believes her daughter and son-in-law committed perjury at the hearing, in an attempt to defame Gloria's good character.

The case was dismissed because of the state's lack of Grandparent Visitation Laws and lack of grandchildren's rights to maintain a relationship with their grandparents. The judge advised both parties to agree on a "liberal and reasonable" schedule of visitation.

Gloria now visits with her grandchildren once a month. Her daughter continues to sabotage what Gloria calls "the originally beautiful relationship I had established with my grandchildren from the time they were born." When Gloria makes her scheduled monthly visits, the children make comments such as: "Mommy said I can't go anyplace with you," or "you can't baby-sit because Mommy doesn't trust you," and "you can't come over unless you are invited." When asked how they are doing in school, their typical response is, "Why do you want to know?"

"My grandchildren no longer show the excitement they once expressed when I was more a part of their lives," Gloria told me. "Now, I am treated more like a visitor. At times they don't even stop what they are doing to greet me when I arrive."

In an effort to cope with the stressful struggles and depression that came with her hardship and to keep from having setbacks with depression, Gloria searched for resources to keep her mind from focusing on the emotional pain she experienced. She attended a bi-monthly support group at Legal Information for Today (LIFT). LIFT provides many services for grandparents raising grandchildren. Gloria did not quite qualify but was welcomed by a support group where members share their stories and discover that they are not alone. In addition to the grandparent support group, LIFT provided Gloria with a social worker who helped prepare her for her day in court.

In addition to LIFT, Gloria attended support groups in her town and several neighboring counties. She met an attorney who introduced her to a psychologist who facilitates a large professional grandparent support group in a neighboring state. The members of that group have not seen their children and/or grandchildren for years or may have never even met their grandchildren. Together, Gloria, the attorney, and the psychologist wrote a proposal that was introduced by a state senator that became a bill that is still in process today. The bill seeks to modify existing laws to give grandparents a more fair and reasonable opportunity to have visitation with their grandchildren who reside in the state. Gloria is working as an advocate, ex-officio lobbyist to see that the state mandates at least one mediation with a court arbitrator before any case is dismissed in court.

After she shifted her energies to legal advocacy, Gloria went back to school and is learning a language and taking computer classes. She is working out regularly at a fitness center and has been able to drop her antidepressants. She is volunteering at the local senior center in her community.

Recently she enrolled in a computer webinar given by the National Committee of Grandparents for Children's Rights (NCGCR) and became a Grandparent Leader and contact person for those who need assistance. She advocates for grandparents and grandchildren on a daily basis. Some of them are raising their grandchildren, and others have no access to their adult children and/or grandchildren. She enjoys "being there" for others like her who are unable to fill the special role that grandparents play in children's lives.

By volunteering in this way, Gloria reports she has been blessed with having relationships with children who love her as much as and perhaps more than her own grandchildren are permitted to. She is glad that she can fill that void in the lives of children who have lost their own grandparents. It fills the emptiness in her own life as well, since she cannot be a loving mother to her own daughter and see her own grandchildren as often as she would like.

Gloria states, "The relationship between a grandparent and grandchild is special, unique, unconditional. I did all that I could to re-establish the relationship I had with my grandchildren.

Although it is not the same as it once was, I will continue to keep trying to be a part of their lives. I am grateful for the opportunity to know my grandchildren and for them to know who I am and how much I love them.

"My wish for my grandchildren is that they know the depth of my love for them. There is nothing I would not do for them. I was always there for them, and always loved them, even when they didn't know it. I will be there for them if they need me. My wish for them is to experience all things that truly matter: beauty, love, creativity, joy and inner peace. My prayer for them is that they laugh often, they win the respect of intelligent people and the affection of other children, appreciate beauty, find the best in others, and leave the world a bit better by service of some sort, whether by a garden patch or a redeemed social condition. I want them to know that even one life has breathed easier because they have lived. This is to have succeeded. May they embrace their potential to do, have, and be whatever they can dream."

By seeking help, participating in support groups, and turning her anger, frustration and pain into legal advocacy, and helping others in need, Gloria is truly a model for others.

Chelsea: Invisible Auntie

Chelsea, 54, is married and has no children. She currently writes young adult fiction and works selling antiques. She grew up privileged in the South. She holds a degree from a prominent university. In previous careers she's been an artist, a medical researcher and an elementary school teacher.

Chelsea has two siblings. The eldest, a brother, has three children: two girls 12 and 15 and a boy 13. She played a big role in their lives that ended several years ago, when her brother's family moved and became devout fundamentalist Christians at his in-law's church. They disapprove of Chelsea's family and religion. In spite of her being Catholic and a teacher, Chelsea's interactions with her brother and his children have been criticized with comments like "You can't understand children, since you've never had any."

Now Auntie Chelsea is not allowed to talk to the children, even when she visits or calls. Since the kids moved, Chelsea has not had one conversation with one child. She received no thank–you cards or calls for gifts that she still sends. Chelsea's widowed father, the children's grandfather, lives in her brother's home and insists that the gifts from Auntie Chelsea be received.

Chelsea is heartbroken, fearing that when her two nieces get married, she'll not be able to see them or attend their weddings. She fears her nephew will move away from the family as soon as he can, but he'll be uncomfortable or unable to get in touch.

"It hurts," Chelsea reports. "These kids are the only next generation in our family. I won't see them grow up and marry. It's like a death in the family. They're in our will. Right now as adults they'll inherit all I have through a trust. At least I can help them someday."

The children are not allowed to use Facebook because parental blocks have been put in place on the computer and television. They aren't allowed to use the phone to call family.

Chelsea sees this as intimidating to children. She tells me she saw personality changes in the kids the last time she visited them. Instead of being outgoing and free, Chelsea felt they were fearful of their parent's judgments and possible punishments if they said more than hello. They don't talk to anyone in her family. They're stifled.

Chelsea considers it punishment to not affirm a kid's ability to connect with family they love. She believes it damages their emotional growth when they can't be comfortable in familial situations. She worries they won't function with confidence in the world. It's heartbreaking and tragic.

How has Chelsea handled this emotionally and spiritually? She says, "I try not to obsess and to accept the things you cannot change as the saying goes. I apply a certain amount of detachment." She holds hope for some time in the future when they are older and perhaps they'll remember her affection for them. "My father does what he can to let the children know we care. Since he's virtually deaf, he uses a speakerphone. I know the kids can overhear us. I use that as a way to get my love through. I call when the kids are home from school and likely to be somewhere within hearing distance. It gives me hope. I hope it makes them happy to know I'll always care.

"There's nothing I can do to change this. I tried strategies to get other family members, i.e., my cousin and sister who are also estranged, to call them, but they failed. Soon my brother and his family will be moving back to this region. That changes aspects of this situation. It'll be easier to occasionally visit with my dad, but there'll be emotional discomfort during visits because of the censorship and the parents not accepting our side of the family."

I asked Chelsea, "If you could share your values, memories, and thoughts with your now invisible nephew and nieces right now, what would they be?"

"I respect religion, but it's being used here as cover to limit the children's interactions with friends and family and to limit their exposure to trying new things as they grow up." Breaking into tears she went on, "This is so hard. I feel they're emotionally imprisoned. Some religious groups isolate members through social restriction. It's unhealthy not to be open. I want them to fearlessly meet new people and have new experiences. It expands you!"

Chelsea's legacy would be that her nieces and nephew stay hopeful: "Some people grow up fine no matter what kind of childhood they had and some don't. I may leave letters for them to read to find out about our side of the family. The movement to link adopted children with their biological parents, and the tremendous efforts by those kids to search out their past, gives me hope that someday when a burning interest about family comes to my nieces and nephews, they'll find me."

Writing is Chelsea's true legacy. She dreams of a day when she can put her nieces' and nephew's names in the dedications to her novels. "I hope one day they'll be in touch again, reading my books, rather than having copies handed to them by an attorney when I die. They'll know I wrote for them. What a wonderful thing that would be!"

An update from Chelsea as this book goes to print: "One of the children has a Facebook page now and responded yes when I offered to friend that child. I've made minimal contact on Facebook as their mother is also on the friends list and can monitor every word. I don't want to lose this slim connection. When they want to, they can contact me. At the current time, there is no direct way to do it. My oldest niece has moved out as an adult and eloped. I have no contact with her or with the third child. The child I did contact hopefully can help me to stay in touch in the future with all the siblings. The parents are still blocking contact where they can, but it's become clear that as the children become independent adults, there will be chances to build a future relationship someday between my house and my nieces and nephew."

These stories are merely the tip of the iceberg that represent the circumstances and the challenges that invisible grandparents face. While not one of the experiences of my interviewees could be labeled as "typical" of the ways the grandparents kept from their grandkids fell into their situation or coped with it, I offer these few in hopes that positive rather than negative energies be put into motion. The next chapter will detail how I found writing letters helped me to be invisible, but not silent, and leave a legacy of my values and memories whether I could be there or not.

INVISIBLE BUT NOT SILENT:
LETTER WRITING AS A HEALING TOOL

In 1956, when I was eleven, I was given a booklet on *How to Write Letters for All Occasions* by Abigail Van Buren of "Dear Abby" fame. Ever since then I've loved writing letters. As I grew up, they were a way of communicating my feelings that was somehow easier or safer than in person. I had a pen pal in Scotland during my middle school years. In my senior year in high school I wrote every day to my first-ever boyfriend, who had gone away to college. Years later, when I asked my mother what she'd done with the box of these love letters I'd left behind when I drove across country to college, I was appalled that she said she had thrown them out. "Sure!" I thought, "but not without reading them first!" I was embarrassed she might have read about my virginal adolescent passion that was likely in them.

When I was at home in my late thirties with two babies, struggling with the work of marriage and motherhood, I exchanged letters with a close girlfriend who was also struggling, but with being single. We thought our correspondence would make a book entitled *Parallel Lives*. I still have a box of our handwritten letters in my garage, and even have had some transcribed.

So it was no accident that, prompted by the mother of my first grandchild, I began to capture my thoughts and feelings by writing letters. Over the past five years I have written dozens of notes, long and short, to both Carter and Annie, some by hand, most by computer. The process of putting words on paper was extremely therapeutic for me. It helped to not only clarify my feelings; but also to release the ones that weren't serving me. By bringing to awareness my perspective on the incomplete grandparenting journey I found myself engaged in, it helped me heal and let go of much of the negative energy I was giving my plight.

As I continued to write, I found myself playing the role a good grandmother might play, were she present. Some letters were about places I might have taken them; others were about family traditions on holidays. Some answered questions I imagined I might be asked at different stages in my grandkids' lives; others were simply my perspective on religion, the news and the politics of the time.

What in Your Bones Do You Want Your Grandchildren to Know?

As I re-read my letters in order to select the collection of sample letters that follow, I was amazed at how my values, "my voice," rang clearly through. I found that indeed I was doing the grandparenting, albeit indirectly, that my destiny had finally prepared me for. I was answering the question Yeshi Neuman asked in a workshop I took on "Conscious Grandparenting," "What in your bones do you want your grandchildren to know?" Here is what I wrote then:

April 23, 2011
Dear Carter and Annie,
I am in a workshop on grandmothering. We were told to write you about "What I know in my bones I want you to know."
I want you to know, especially now at ages 9 and 11 before those growing up-teenage hormones hit you, is:
#1 that you are extremely smart, that your good looks and intelligence come in large part from the father you may never get to see and acknowledge, and #2 that you can do anything you set your mind to. "Smart" does not always have to mean "good in school." You can master anything you have a passion for, that you love to do, and you can become successful at it.
#3 I want you to know that the kindness and thoughtfulness I've witnessed in Carter the few times I've seen him comes from his wonderful mom Lily, and the dad he's come to know in John.
I love you. As your genetic grandmother, the mother

*of your biological father Brad, I know that he holds a lot
of love in his heart for both of you, but right now he has
come to hide it.*

Love,

Grandma Pat

*P.S. I also have to tell you one important thing I forgot:
Beer, wine and the hard stuff are NOT good lubricants.
They don't really make things run more smoothly, or
life a little lighter, though it may seem like they do for a
short time. Using drugs or alcohol is not using you! They
mask your talented, nice, pure, creative self. And they are
chemicals that can get addictive and be difficult to stop.
Though you probably will, I hope you never use them. If
I could do anything to prevent addictions in the world, I
would.*

Writing Letters to Save
and Share Someday (SSS Letters)

It is my sincere hope that the guidelines for letter writing and the
collection of sample letters in the next chapter will inspire other
visible and invisible grandparents to compose and collect their
own missives. May it help us all rise above difficult circumstances
and provide a beacon for future generations that will guide their
way. It is my hope that letter writing will help us all "hold the high
watch" by having positive aspirations for our children. They are
our future as Whitney Houston sings. Let's put a positive vibration
out there.

There is no one way to write an Invisible Grandparent letter.
Some may be one paragraph in your own handwriting; others
might be computer-generated and pages long, or simply a few lines
on a birthday card or postcard. While modeling proper grammar
and spelling where possible, we are not "grading" these letters like
in school. Move the words onto the page that say what you want
to say as quickly as possible without censoring yourself. You can

always edit or rewrite before you save or release a letter, if you choose to do so.

If you are a completely invisible or truly transparent grandparent, it may be difficult to envision or even name the child. Say that in your first sentence, and then make up a name if you would like. Perhaps you might tell the child why you have chosen that particular first name and perhaps something about the history of your own name.

You might imagine a return letter and your own response to it. You might make up imaginary questions a child of that age might ask, then write a letter answering them at the age they are, or some stage in their lives in the future. Write to your one-year-old, six-year-old, ten-year-old, teenager or young adult as *if* they could "get" the message in your words.

Include pictures of yourself, of the places you would have taken them, and programs or souvenirs from events in your life. Share your perspective on life, the seasons, virtually anything. Tell them about yourself, your family history, past traditions and then save them! If necessary make believe, or genuinely hope that someday the child will actually receive and read your letters. Make a special scrapbook, decorate a box for them, or create electronic files that include pictures and music. By the time you are done, likely never, you could fill a virtual trunk with the gift of your very own thoughts that you'd like to pass on. The possibilities are endless.

Writing Said but Never Send (SSS) Letters

Writing letters I knew I would never send, gave me an opportunity to vent my feelings in ways little else could. In *My Back-Story* you read my first "Say it but Never Send it" (SNS) letter, *Christmas Hurts*. Below is another SNS letter I wrote a year later after I'd fully comprehended the finality of my situation and felt my invisibility was being etched into stone. I needed to dump my feelings of resentment and downright anger about the mother who was blocking me from seeing my grandchild.

By writing some of these directly to the mother who was keeping me from seeing her child, I discharged feelings that might, if not expressed, have produced stress-related illnesses in my body. This process and the releasing I did afterward contributed to my healing, which is still going on. Grief takes a long time to be released fully, but this helped open the door.

Thursday, December 27, 2007
Dear Suzie:

If guilt would work to get you to allow me to be part of your family, I would secretly instill it in your food. I'd dish it out in big scoops and top it with sprinkles that give you some sense of the seemingly endless hole of sadness that I have had in my heart for weeks as the Christmas season began and now thankfully has almost passed.

How dare you deprive the experience of "Grandma Pat" from the life of the five-year-old little girl whose gene pool I have directly contributed to! Mea culpa. What have I done to deserve this?"

I parented as best I could the young man that you once were in love with. I watched him, as you did, slide down the hill of his own lack of self-esteem, fueled first by pot and alcohol, and then meth-fucking amphetamine!

My prayer is that when his daughter is able to make choices of the kind he faced, she makes good ones. That she escapes dependency on anything but her own strength, imagination and talent to go after her dreams! I truly hope that she reaches for something greater than what appears before her, applies herself and goes for it, as apparently her father did not. Yet.

Dammit Suzie, I wish you could feel my pain and confusion, open your heart and mind, and allow me in Annie 's life. I want to do that now, as she develops, not then, when she is 18 or 23 or 33 and goes on some soap-opera-induced search for her roots. She deserves the experiences only someone like me could provide for her. And you do, too. The more people that children get parenting from, the more role models they have for growing up adult, the better.

Can you even imagine how I felt when Julie, my not favorite person in the world anyway, told me at Thanksgiving that you'd asked that I not even have your new address?

"Why?" I asked, and Julie mumbled, "Suzie said you were 'too intense!' "

Well, intensity be damned, it took every ounce of restraint on my part to not to say to Julie "and you're not?" The judgment and blame I felt from both Sam and Julie at that time was palpable. Sam never agreed with the way I did anything, much less parented. It was one of the reasons I left him.

I can't write this much longer. I want to go to the gym and walk the treadmill with music between my ears, hoping that will wipe away this grief.

Yet right now I feel compelled to get brave enough to vomit out just a few more words of my own guilt, the heart-wrenching "wish I'ds" and "if onlys" and "I should'ves" that would erase all the bad choices Brad made since he was 6, but escalated at 15. I want to wish him into walking a different path right now, not taking us all down the road to hell that addiction can. Mothers merely want their child to realize how great he or she is on their own ... without chemically induced brainpower. Every mother yearns, as I do for Brad, for him to believe in his own looks, his intelligence, his talents, his ability to love and be loved in return.

All right, I admit I was a mom who "chose" to "rear" her boys only in summers and on holiday weeks off from school, from when they were 6 and 8, to 16 and 18 I chose to let them get the school year kind of family: the

*Pop Warner football and Boy Scout type of family that
I didn't think I was capable of, with two people I really
didn't like.*

*And yes, there was that adult party when they were
15 and 13, and Larry's son 16. We told them they could
have one beer, not realizing that more behind parents'
backs would be in order. But dammit! My guilt over
not being able to say "no" more often when they were
little, for running away from their father's anger and his
overprotection, as well as the empty void that the initial
love we once had turned into, doesn't help. I know that
guilt is the gift that keeps on giving and won't get you
anywhere. Regrets won't change anything.*

*I must move on. I must find important distracting
work to get into, and pray all day every day as I do, that
soon, very soon, my firstborn will have had enough of
this last bad choice of crystal meth. I want to will him
to have an "Alcoholics Anonymous Bill Wilson lightning
bolt breakthrough," as my husband had years ago, for an
addiction I'd blinded myself from seeing for so long.*

*So, Suzie, please continue to BE the wonderful mother
you are to your growing girl/woman without me. And
please know at least, that the tears I am shedding at this
very moment are not for naught. They free me of the
toxins of grief and negative energy unexpressed.*

*I can move on. Surrendering to this must be one of
the challenges I am destined to face, on my own road to
enlightenment. But God it sure isn't fun!*

Happy New Year Suzie. Really. I mean it.

Love, Invisible Grandma Pat

I have put the memory of those few horrid months five years
ago far behind me. I'm glad to report that my son has moved
beyond that addiction and the bad choices that marked that period
in his life.

Hopefully, this particular letter marked the "bottom" of my experiences as a mother and grandmother.

In workshops I give on *Invisible Grandparenting: Healing Separation*, I ask participants to write the letter they would never send, not necessarily to the child, but perhaps to the person or cultural institution blocking them from being a fully visible grandparent. Doing this can work in any situation where a misunderstanding or separation from a loved one, is out of your own hands.

I tell them to forget about grammar and spelling, that there is no formula for this process, no one way to express themselves. I urge they write quickly as possible, and not censor their thoughts. For the moment judgments, shame and blame are okay, we examine and discard them later. And, of course, I encourage they feel the feelings and notice where in their body they occur. When the heart opens tears flow. Crying is not only normal, it is welcomed.

These are a few "Said but Never Send" (SNS)" letters written by invisible grandparents in workshops I've conducted.

> Dear _____:
> We were always so close, had such a nice relationship. I never imagined a riff like this could come between us. Although you have explained your reasons to me why you can't have us as part of your life, I still don't get it.
>
> At first I respected your wish for "space" believing it was temporary and would pass over. But this has gone on way too long. And now the problem is created by you. You are showing a very bad example to your daughter that relationships are not worth saving. For you it's easier to just throw people away, not to work on healing, just stuff your emotions and go on to the next.
>
> You are so wrong! This is terrible behavior and has broken up our entire family. You are being selfish, arrogant and immature.
>
> Get over it!

⊡ ⊞ ⊡

Dear _____,

I feel so left out! I understand you're hormonally challenged and you want your space, but I haven't seen you or my grandbaby for weeks just to visit and connect with, and honestly I wish you were someone else. After buying a fancy car with super life-saving devices so your child would be safe with me, I think she's only ridden with me once. And by the way, thanks for bringing me take-out when I was sick.

P.S. Don't hang on so tight! Even if she's your only child you'll squeeze the life out of her! But that's not likely, she's too strong!

Love, Mom

◦ ▪ ◦

Dear _____,

How dare you, you f---ing bitch, keep my grandkids from me! The ones I practically raised for three years before you snuck back in the door. I once told you I believed any difference we had could be resolved through love and respect. However, I didn't know what a controlling bitch you are! The stuff you do to my grandkids is absolutely cruel. Kids don't get anything positive from three-hour time-outs because they looked at you the wrong way.

I hope to the Great Spirit—Father—Mother—God that you realize this soon. Calling me a liar and a fake because you just can't wrap your head around the fact that someone could honestly forgive the nasty things you've done just doesn't cut it for me.

◦ ▪ ◦

Release: Transform Negative Energy to Forgiveness

While writing SNS letters gave me some sense of satisfaction, a large part of me needed to shake off the negative energy I'd expressed. I wanted to dissolve or diffuse it, make it go away. I had participated in many a "burning bowl" ceremony on New Year's Eves, so I decided to physically crumple up and burn some SNS letters that I'd printed, while I literally danced in the moonlight to Janis Joplin's song "Piece of My Heart."

It was cathartic. It helped me to have more patience with my situation, to realize that I was not in control, and could only get on with my own life. In workshops we actually use flash paper as we release our SNS sentiments.

Afterward I conduct a guided visualization that my therapist had used with me, to continue the release. I ask the participants to close their eyes, sit quietly and focus on their breathing. Then I very slowly I invite them to relax each part of their body. I ask them to imagine they are standing somewhere in nature near a bubbling brook. I suggest they take each of their harsh feelings one at a time, and imagine they can place them on a leaf that floats down stream and disappears.

As we envision these negative feeling disappearing and disintegrating, I recommend we stop beating ourselves up for having them, accept that "what is, is," and move toward forgiveness of the persons, places and things that we cannot control.

To wind up the session I read a poem titled, "FLOW."

FLOW

Be
As water is
Without friction

Flow around the edges
Of those within your path
Surround within your ever-moving depths
Those who come to rest there
Enfold them
While never for a moment holding on.

Accept whatever distance
Others are moved within your flow.
Be with them gently

As far as they allow your strength to take them
And fill with your own being
The remaining space when they are left behind.

When dropping down life's rapids
Froth and bubble into fragments if you must,
Knowing that the one of you now many
Will just as many times be one again.

And when you've gone as far as you can go
Quietly await your next beginning.

~Anonymous

MY LEGACY OF LETTERS AND LIFE LESSONS

It was very difficult to select letters for this book from the collection I've written. Even more difficult was sorting them into meaningful categories. When themes emerged, there was considerable overlap. Chronological order didn't work. Many letters fit more than one category.

I found myself writing most of the letters to Annie, the granddaughter that is truly invisible to me, and fewer directed to Carter, who I now see and speak to occasionally. Many of the more recent letters I directed to both of them. Some specifically to be "Said but Never Sent" were directed to Suzie, the mother who is blocking me from seeing Annie. Others I wrote to "the Universe" spouting off my thoughts and feelings at the time.

As an academically trained writer, I realized early on that many of my letters were long, verbose, and often not age-appropriate. Therefore I developed a practice of paraphrasing and explaining "big words" not understandable to a 9- or 10-year-old. I even thought of labeling some letters "PG" or "PG-13" or "R" like in the movies. My intention, however, was merely that they be read someday. I suspect my grandchildren might be quite adult and able to receive and understand these if and when they discover this legacy in letters.

As I reviewed the letters I surprised myself when I became aware of hidden "Life Lessons" within messages on other subjects. Since my major goal in writing these letters was to leave a legacy of what I had learned for my grandchildren, I highlighted these **LIFE LESSONS** in this first edition.

What follows are categories for letters I wrote over the past five years. They are not all-inclusive. The first section continues to unravel the circumstances that led to my invisibility. These samples are merely suggestions of the types of things any grandparent might want their grandkids to know. They were inspired by daily events in my life, as well as questions I imagined my grandchildren might ask me at various ages and stages in their own lives.

Some are based on the different roles that grandparents play in young people's lives. As you peruse my legacy, may you be encouraged to devise your own.

My Invisibility Continued
Out of Sight, Out of Mind? Not Really.

February 6, 2009
Dear Annie & Carter,
*   I am visiting old friends in Paradise where I used to live. Yup, Paradise is really the name of this small kind of redneck town in the hills above Chico, in California's central valley. In fact my address was "1269 Storybook Lane, zip code 95969." Can you believe that? Remember to ask me for another letter about why 69 is a lucky number for me.*
*   Anyway my friends Bob and Annie met and married twenty years ago when they each had grown children. When you walk up the path through their garden to the house you see this sign:*

Grand Kids Welcome
Cuddles and giggles
Cookies and treats
Days spent at grandma's
Are always so sweet!

*   A wooden frame for the doorknocker on the front door has two cutesey balding bespectacled "old people" with curly wires for hair that reads* Grandpa and Grandma's House. *Inside every nook and cranny of their tiny house there are many, many framed pictures of beautiful babies, young people and growing families in every room at Christmas, weddings, Halloween, etc. I counted literally 73 framed photos! The kitchen smells like chocolate chip*

cookies were just out of the oven.

You know what? All of this made me feel a little sick. Yes, I'm happy for them, but I'm actually jealous of the connections and the good times in these carefully chosen pictures show on their walls. While there is something comforting about this "typical" grandparent's house, it makes me feel creepy. Creepy because my house doesn't have any, not one, picture of either of you up for display. It isn't that I don't have any, I've got plenty from when Annie was 1-4, or when I first met Carter when he was 5 months old, and the times since that I can count on my hands that I've visited Lily and her now family of five. I just don't advertise what I can't have. I keep the reminders of you out of sight; but unfortunately that doesn't keep you out of mind.

As Brad and his brother Brian grew up, I was a different kind of parent. I got divorced when they were two and four. After a year of shuffling them between two houses every other week, with their father's permission, I took a dream job on the West coast, and paid child support. I had your father and his brother in Paradise every summer and most school vacations, starting when they were six and eight. I was actually more of an "Auntie Mame" or "grandma mom" then. I was lucky to have the fun times, and didn't have to help with the homework or make you do chores. I've always been grateful to their stepmom Julie for what a good mother she was. Of course I missed all the Pop Warner football games, and soccer, and boy scouts and such; but I don't think I would've been very good at that.

So now I find it funny that I am once again "not typical" as a grandparent. The word I came up with is "invisible." It means, as many people believe about angels, that our thoughts and spirits are with you, wishing for you the best, whether we can be there or not.

So I'm writing you these letters (or setting up a regular blog) to leave some of me for you someday. That's what a legacy is. I decided to get as close to the truths I'd like to tell you about life, about what I know I know and want to share with you. Hopefully someday you'll have the inclination to read them.

There is much about the past that contributes to your present moment. That is what this compilation is about: me talking out loud to my very real grandchildren that I don't get to see. We'll get to getting closer to that present moment in future letters about metaphysical principles to be designated for when you are older.

I'm swallowing hard right now. This is going to be quite a challenge that most in-person grandparents don't even get to do. Can I do it? Voice my truths, the things I would say like no one else can? Coming from the depths of my love and the worst of my past circumstances, and voiced so a ten-year-old could understand it?

Sure I can. O.K. Do it Pat.

Carter and Annie … have a great day. Find something special to do and let me know what that is, eh?

Love,
Grandma Pat

◻ ◫ ◻

Partially Visible Grandparenting Can Hurt Too

July 28, 2009
Dear Muse,

I had a difficult night. I dreamt I was trapped on the first floor of a small tall narrow apartment building in NYC that had only a winding staircase and one of those iron-gated elevators. Both were blocked. All kinds of strange people had gone up before me but for some reason I could not. The air smelled of varnish because workmen were removing some from the ornate woodworking around the doorways to get down to the original surface of the wood.

I don't know what the dream means, but it felt like there was no way up or out. This mirrored the crushed feeling I had this morning. I tossed and turned all night with self-questioning, writhing with disappointment about the decision Lily made to not let me take Carter to the Harry Potter Hogwarts dinner and movie that the library where I'm house-sitting is holding. I understand that his brother, who is five, wouldn't know why he couldn't go and feel left out (she thinks it'd be too scary for him). I offered a "play date" for some future special activity with me. But she also said she wouldn't fully feel comfortable letting either of them drive with me all of 2.5 miles to get the brownies I'd forgotten and bring them to the lake. Fooey!

Once again I took it personally. I felt rejected and like I'm not being trusted. This is certainly not as great as the level that made my other grandchild's mom block me from participating in Annie's life, No this isn't even close. But the feelings are way too familiar. Dreams of being blocked from rising above are all too close to home.

Lily is such a good mom that I bowed to her needs and was actually surprised that Carter didn't throw a fit. Either he didn't really understand and didn't want to go, or he knows how to listen to his mother and do what she says is best. (That was different than how my kids would've reacted!) Any way you look at it, Carter's reaction was a good thing. I am the one that needed to "let go." But once again, I was unable to shake the sadness at being kept from being the grandmother I want to be.

Invisible grandparenting hurts; but being partially visible can hurt too. This goes deep for me. It may have something to do with the mothering, by choice, I never did with both my sons. I thought I'd paid my dollars and dues in years of therapy, and had long gotten over guilt from the separation from my own kids that I brought on when I arranged their bi-coastal custody agreement at ages 6 and 8 with their father. They spent school years in New York, summers and vacations with me in California. In spite of accusations of "abandonment" from some of my friends who had their psychological jargon down, I think all four parents and step-parents would agree that this was the best possible way to raise Brad and Brian.

The carried feelings from these very deep losses probably can't be made up for by taking one child to what I think would be an exciting event. So, I went to the Hogwarts dinner by myself. I borrowed a multicolored feather duster I'd given Lily, and disguised myself as a fairy godmother. I blessed all the children young and old with good luck and told them it was a magic wand.

May whatever I've learned about creating good memories rub off on Carter and Annie invisibly. Is that so bad? Perhaps all I really wanted to do was witness being a child again.

Love,
Invisible "Mother-in-Law" Pat

July 29th—P.S. Now I realize that Lily was right. Her decision kept Carter from being uncomfortable. The other kids were older than he was and he hadn't read the Harry Potter books yet, because of his dyslexia problem in school. **LIFE LESSON: Giving in and letting go does work, sometimes.**

Watch Out for Expectations

October 24, 2009
Dear Annie,
This is another letter I'm writing while crying. Tears can be a good thing sometimes when you're sad. Crying can be okay, especially when there is someone to hold you who understands you. I wish I could be that person for you. Larry is there for me like that. I am so lucky to have a husband who listens and understands and supports me no matter what.

There were two reasons for my tears. The first is your birthday. Seven! I haven't seen you since you were four! How tall you must be, and how long that blonde hair could be! Is it? I'm happy for you. What made me cry, though, was that I didn't realize it was October 24ᵗʰ until today (!) when I saw the date. It came as a shock because I am in Atlanta at a conference and was about to lead a workshop on Invisible Grandparenting. Funny, I think it was no accident that it was your birthday.

This conference is a gathering of "Crones, wise older women," from age 45 to 95! The 200 women here are not all your typical granny types. They come in all shapes and sizes, some even in wheelchairs. Every year these older women from all over the country get together and tell stories about heartaches and celebrations in their lives. In the opening ceremonies they bring in energy or spirits from the four directions: North, South, East and West, and dance and drum like Native Americans do. One 95-year-old lady even told dirty jokes in the "follies," the talent show they had.

The other reason I was crying was that when some of them talked about how they take their grandchildren shopping for school clothes, or on trips to faraway places, or how smart and successful many of their now

*grownup grandchildren are, it was hard for me. I don't
have anything to brag about you. If I made something up,
what might that be?*

*But guess what? Also sad is that not one person,
showed up for my workshop! I was going to have
them write letters like these that I save for you, to
grandchildren they might not be able to see for all kinds
of reasons, including even if a baby died or was given up
for adoption. The purpose was to have them express their
good wishes for that child and help them heal their hurts.
I was also going to have the other grandmothers write
about the mad, angry, vengeful feelings they have about
why this happened. Then we would crumple up and
destroy these letters and let the negative feelings go.*

*Lots of people came up to me and told me how
important what I was doing was, for all the other
grandmas like me; but not one of them who read the
program or heard my pitch for it walked into the room.
Instead they took workshops on laughing yoga, or
cleansing tonics to purify the body. I had looked forward
to this and was really disappointed.* **LIFE LESSON: I think
it told me something about an-tic-i-pation and having
expectations. You can plan for things, but don't count on
the outcome.** *I got over it, but it felt weird.*

*So that's enough for today. It's getting near winter.
Even in Atlanta it was cold in the mornings. The leaves on
the trees were changing into bright colors.*

Love,
Grandma Pat

▷   ▷▷   ▷

Your Father Showed Up!

November 30, 2008
Dear Annie,

I had the surprise of my life on Thanksgiving! Your father, who none of us had heard from, actually showed up! It had been 18 months, a year and a half since I'd seen or heard from him. His brother the Navy Seal called and said he'd be a little late because he was bringing a friend. We assumed a girl. When the doorbell rang and Brad walked in, no one, especially me, expected to see him. I almost had forgotten what he looked like. The first thing he said was, "I would've called you mom, but I wanted to see the look on your face, and give you a heart attack!"

I'm sure he saw the tears in my eyes. I put my hands to my heart and hugged him. He slipped right into greeting his cousins and sitting around talking about the tree-cutting service he is working for in the mountains, and how he's in training to be a ski patrol for the winter. No one really addressed his long absence, or even mentioned your name. I guess none of us, Brad at the top of the list were ready to talk about it then and just let it go. Today, I wonder how or even if we will ever talk about what we'd all really like to know. Or if it's better to just "let go, and let bygones be bygones." We'll see.

I really know deep inside how much he still loves you, and wish you could've seen him too. But oh well, that's just not how things are right now, are they?

Love,
Grandma Pat

Your Father Called Today

January 4, 2010
Dear Annie,

Funny, just after I finished writing you yesterday, your father called! When I saw his name appear on my cell phone my heart skipped a beat. I had gotten an address from him at Thanksgiving, a post office box in a town near the ski resort he works at. I texted him five days before Christmas and told him a package was there, and he texted me back "tx."

No call at Christmas, no call at New Year's like he used to do when he was a teenager. No thank you Mom for the candy (almond English toffee that we used to make every year), and the Mr. Magorium's Wonder Emporium *video, and the other little stocking stuffers I put in his package. I'd even included a pair of my signature Laurel Burch sox for his girlfriend that I've only heard about. It wasn't until January 3rd that I heard from him.*

It hurt me that he didn't call on Christmas day because his brother told me he had heard from him. So I "didn't go there" into the sadness or the anger at him for being so insensitive; because there were other Christmases that both he and your granddad from New York (his father that you do see), didn't even know where he was or if he was alive. Back then to get through the holidays, I just prayed that he was okay and tried not to think about it.

Today he sounded alert and good. He told me he was working two jobs, and that just this week he'd had time to drive down to that post office and get his package. I just said "oh" or some such. Brad always was a man of few words, so I didn't complain. I just asked him questions about his job and how cold it must be up there and stuff.

There are always long pauses when I talk to Brad on the phone. It's like he doesn't want to hang up, but doesn't know what else to say and I don't know what to ask. It's weird. Sometimes I think it's a guy thing. Girlfriends were always so much easier for me to talk to.

Communicating with Brad is like pulling teeth sometimes. That's an expression people use about people who don't say much and have to be urged to say things. I bet you're not like that. I remember that at four you were very verbal and had all sorts of things to say. In fact that is the hardest part about writing these letters. It's so one-way. I never get to hear what you'd write or say back.

Oh well, like at Thanksgiving and Christmas, **LIFE LESSON: I just am grateful for the little things, and bite my tongue sometimes to keep from saying anything negative directly because that usually doesn't help.**

Are you headed back to school today? Probably.

I love you. Have fun.

Grandma Pat

▫ ◻ ▫

Oh the Places We Would Go!
Postcard Memories: Santa Barbara

August 23, 2008
Dear Carter & Annie,

I am house-sitting for your great-aunt my sister Joan, in Santa Barbara, California. This town on the edge of the Pacific ocean, at the foot of a range of beautiful green mountains, is one of, no THE most beautiful place I have ever visited. Spanish white stucco buildings with their red tiled roofs are everywhere, even the McDonalds and the Albertson's supermarket up on the road they call "the mesa" because the houses are built on a bluff or plateau above the ocean, all look the same.

I realize that I am using big words sometimes. Perhaps when I do, you can look up the words in a dictionary. That's a big book with the words and what they mean in them. You can get to one on the computer too. Let me know which words you missed or didn't understand.

Your father Brad and his brother Brian came to Santa Barbara to visit my sister every summer from when they were six and eight, till when they graduated high school. Yesterday I was on Hendry's Beach watching the little kids with boogie boards ride the waves and come out smiling and screaming. One of them looked just like they did years ago. I will try to find pictures of back then, and put them with this letter. One year, we moved from Aunt Joan's house because she didn't have cable TV (and she was also a clean freak) in to a motel around the corner with a pool, because the Olympics were on. We watched them every night after a day in the sun.

Are you watching the 2008 Olympics from China? Which parts do you like best? Brian used to love the swimming and the running. He started doing sit-ups every morning when he was in first grade. And yes, he became a winning triathelete (another word for you to look up) and now he is a Navy Seal. That is one of our country's strongest, finest, best-trained military athletes. Have you heard of them? Let me know. Girls cannot become Navy Seals, but they can and do run, race, play and win at sports of all kinds. Do you do any of these things? Your mom was on a winning volleyball team in high school.

I have to stop now because I am going to a 3-D movie of a circus "Cirque du Soleil" in Santa Barbara's Arlington Theatre. Your father and Brian loved that theatre. We saw The Lion King there when it first came out. It has Spanish architecture even inside. The side balconies are little stucco houses with lights shining through tiny windows from real rooms. They have balconies that people used to sit on. On the wall are pictures with signed autographs of old movie stars from Gone with the Wind and The Wizard of Oz at the openings of those movies made more than 70 years ago.

The ceiling has stars that really twinkle on it, and a moon that changes with the seasons. The bathroom is bigger than my living room, and has a lobby with tall gold ornate mirrors and colorful flags hanging from the ceiling. The walls are painted with murals of men in tight-fitting tuxedos and women in long black flowing dresses, Flamenco dancing and waving pretty fans.

Oh how I wish you were here. More another day. Please write back, as little or as much as you can.

I love you. Grandma Pat

▣ ▦ ▣

Birthday I.O.U.'s

August 23, 2008
Dear Annie,
    Your 10th birthday! You've been growing up a full decade! I can hardly imagine what you must look like, or what type of birthday party you and your very creative mother have planned. The last one I went to, you were three. It was ninety degrees outside, held in a park and the kids all waded in a tiny creek. You got a green and yellow ride-em tractor just your size.

    Remember last year on your "brother's" 11th birthday, I told you your biological father gave me another grandchild who lives on the East coast in rolling farm country? I guess that makes him your brother (or is it stepbrother?). Maybe there's another word for it. His name is Carter.

    Anyway, Carter's mom is married now, and he has a brother and a sister. He knows he's adopted now, and that I am his "real" grandma, so I get to send presents and sign them Grandma. He has a problem with reading called dyslexia where you get words mixed up, so I don't send books like I used to anymore.

    Last year on his 11th birthday I made him this "I.O.U. Card Redeemable at an Imaginary Future Date." It had an air view photo of the Monterey Peninsula and then snapshots of all the places within ten minutes of my home that I'd like to take him (and you!) someday: kayaking in the Elkhorn Slough seeing sea otters close-up, the Aquarium, hiking in Big Sur and having lunch on the beach near Lovers Point in Pacific Grove.

    If I could send you a card like that, it would include all of the above, as well as some girly lunch at a fancy restaurant with a view of the ocean. I still remember the time my grandmother took me to The Top of the Sixes

in a skyscraper in New York City for my 13ᵗʰ birthday.
Hmmm...put that on your list of possibilities.

LIFE LESSON: What are birthdays for, really? They
are a reminder of time. Time that passes for all of us, no
matter how old we are. Our lives and bodies grow and
change as we mature from that first day we arrived on
this planet when our moms gave birth to us. *Kids have*
parties and give each other presents, but when I go to
birthday parties, I like to give something to the moms
because they are the ones who carried us for nine months
and then "pushed us out" in childbirth. I usually give
bubble bath or lingerie or something really feminine.

Enjoy your birthday. On my 30ᵗʰ, one of my friends told
me to **LIFE LESSON: "create your own birthday." She**
said not to wait for family or friends to surprise you...
just find some good things and do them for yourself. *I*
always try get a massage, sometimes even at Esalen in
Big Sur, and then have lunch with some special women
friends. I wonder what you will choose to do, as you get
older.

Love,
Invisible Grandma Pat

◧ ⬓ ◨

A Christmas Trip to Radio City NYC

November 21, 2010
Dear Annie & Carter,

Ooooh! I just finished reading the Arts & Leisure section of The Sunday New York Times. *I always read that first, before that paper's steaming intelligent analysis of current events. I swear reading* The New York Times *raises my IQ ten points. But somehow "the arts" draw my attention first, before all the depressing news about war and hurricanes and earthquakes and epidemics. This Sunday's theatre-movie-dance sections made me yearn to be closer to you, and richer! I would take you to Manhattan. Want to know what we'd do?*

We'd take the train down the Hudson and stay in a cool hotel. Maybe even a bed & breakfast in SOHO (that's an artsy type district). The first day we'd go see the Christmas tree in Rockefeller Plaza, yes, that's the one rock stars often perform in front of on "The Today Show." Then we'd watch the ice skaters in Rockefeller Center, and maybe even rent some skates and actually do that. Perhaps we'd walk up to Central Park Zoo, or go to the Planetarium and see a light show. By evening after dinner, perhaps at Nirvana in a Tent that has a view of all of Central Park, I'd have gotten great tickets to Radio City Music Hall for The Rockettes' Christmas performance.

Wow, I just looked at the moving "preview" of this show on its website (www.radiocitychristmas.com)! My grandmother took me to see that Christmas show, a long long time ago when I was your age. I don't remember it being like this; it's even MORE spectacular. I will never forget how the dancers' legs looked: all the same and doing the same motions all at once. I took dance lessons, but could never do anything like that. Then at the end, I remember all this steam covered the stage and Santa's sleigh comes in. It was really magical.

Well, that is just the beginning of all the places we would go, IF I were your visible grandma. Right now, I'll keep wishing and wonder about all the Christmas traditions your parents are putting into your memory banks. I love you.

Grandma Pat

P.S. As I was humming this tune: "City sidewalks, busy sidewalks dressed in holiday style, in the air there's a feeling of Christmas," my heart just jumped. As I looked on the website at the cities for the national tour of the Radio City Christmas show this holiday season, the town Annie lives in is on it! I guess I'll just "intend" that Suzie take her whole family. Sigh! Sure wish I could be there to see your faces.

◩ ◪ ◩

Spike Jonz's Where The Wild Things Are—Too Wild?

January 20, 2010
Dear Annie & Carter,

*   I just saw a movie that I thought it would be fun to take you to, if you were around.* Where the Wild Things Are *was a picture book that your father Brad and Uncle Brian, and probably every kid on the block had and loved. It was written and illustrated by Maurice Sendak in 1963, and finally made into a movie this year. It wasn't a cartoon movie. The characters were actors playing animals in these huge furry feathery costumes. The expressions on their faces and voices were really real.*

*   Have you read the storybook? It has very very few words. It's about a little boy who gets punished by his mother for dressing up and making a mess in his house, and then talking back to her when she calls him "wild thing." That night in his imagination, his room turns into a jungle and he gets whisked away on a ship to an island with all these big monsters. At first they scare him, until he looks them in they eye and says, "Be still!" Then he tames them with a magic trick. They make him king and he has great fun with them until he gets lonely and hungry, and wants to go home. Which he does.*

*   Well the movie director, Spike Jonze, really had to stretch that short story into a 120-minute movie, and I had some issues with it. I wish I could've seen it with you first, before I give you my opinion. Here goes. I'd have asked you what part you liked best, and which character you liked or didn't like. I'd have loved to hear your answer to my questions about what message you think the moviemaker wanted to get across.*

*   But here goes my take: I felt it was too negative and violent. Annie, I remember when your mother and I had to take you out of the movie* Ratatouille, *because*

it scared you. In Wild Things, *I thought the struggle between the brother and his sister was overdone. The snowball fight and another battle on the island were not things I'd like to see modeled for kids like you. However, this doesn't even come close to all the violence on television, especially in the news. I suppose I can't protect you from images like this. I'd sure like the opportunity to talk about them with you, though.*

Well here's the link for the trailer for the movie. It has lots of pictures of the wonderful animals. If I could, I'd send you a DVD of it for Valentine's Day. (wherethewildthingsare.warnerbros.com)

Love, Your wannabe screenwriter Grandmother Pat

◻ ▣ ◻

Sleeping Beauty—*Out of Date?*

January 25, 2010
Dear Annie and Carter,

Today I went to a theatrical performance of Sleeping Beauty *all by myself. I wanted to be with children and watch how they'd react to seeing real people act out that famous fairy tale. I wanted to feel like a child again myself. I think that is why so many people love being with their grandchildren and doing special things with them.*

It was sold out. One family, with girls all dressed up in velvet dresses and boys in white shirts & bow ties, hadn't gotten tickets ahead and were turned away. But I waited for "standing room only" at this tiny theatre at Monterey Peninsula College till everyone arrived, and got the last seat. I sat next to a six-year-old boy who told me that his first-grade teacher was playing the good witch. She was really really funny and the actors combined singing rock n' roll songs with the story. You'd have loved it.

One part of the story surprised me however. I still have the red hardcover Grimm's Fairy Tales *book my grandmother gave me when I was in the fifth grade. But I had forgotten all of the parts of* Sleeping Beauty *since I first read it over 60 years ago. The narrator of the play said at the beginning that the king and queen were very very sad, and the whole kingdom wept and was very very sad too, because they were unable to have a child. Over and over, they moaned and groaned and lamented about not having a baby.*

I thought this was a little overdone and out of date. **LIFE LESSON: There are lots of couples today that choose not to have children, and get on with their lives just fine.** *Some might have medical reasons for not getting pregnant. They get used to the idea and either adopt a baby or do other things to occupy their free time. But I* *guess that wasn't how it was back then, especially when the mom and dad were a king and queen with a whole kingdom to run and pass on to their children.*

So I just let that go, and enjoyed the rest of the show with the other kids and parents.

Good day, my sleeping beauty!

Love, your still Invisible Grandma Pat

Love, Sex and Marriage
You Were Married Three Times, Grandma. Why?

January 26, 2010
Dear Annie and Carter,

I can hear you asking me, "You were married three times, Grandma. Why?"

"Great question," I'd reply "How much time do you have and what would you like to know?"

Well, since this is to the seven-year-old you, and shorter is better, I'll give you the "in a nutshell" version first. Writing it will help me remember exactly what I learned from each marriage. I'll try to tell you why I fell in love and married each time, as well as why I left. And to be fair, I'll tell you the gifts each of these men were to my life.

Hmmm, since in my career I was a sex educator, and the language I used from an early age is rather "adult," I may do a version to you at 7 with a "G" rating, and after it's done, decide to put it in a pile labeled "PG-13," save it with others for when you'd be more ready to hear them, perhaps "PG-17" or another "R" rated version, for say age 27.

The two later versions may have sexual images and bad words; but they will be the truth as I see it. Lucky for me, I've never experienced any physical violence, so we don't have to worry about rating that like in far too many movies, will we?

Marriage #1—Pete Hanson

And yes, I still use his last name. I was twenty. It was the summer after my junior year in college in California. I'd been sent to Chico State on an "exchange" program by my school in New Jersey. I never thought I would go away to college like my other high school friends did, because my family couldn't afford to send me.

I met Pete in 1964 in the dining hall where I worked pouring orange juice into little glasses every morning at 6 a.m. He was a track star, a graduate student and music major. He played clarinet and saxophone. He was very smart and said the most profound (deep) things in my English novel class. Also, he was rather unusual looking. At 23 his bright blonde hair was already balding and he combed it back.

In retrospect (me looking backward from now), I fell in love with his looks and his brain, and we got married because that's what you did then. I didn't really want to move back to New Jersey, and he didn't want to go to his first teaching job in a small town in the Sierras alone. We had a beautiful wedding on August 25th 1964, in the church at First and Normal Streets on the Chico State campus. My mother and two sisters drove across the country in a Volkswagen van for the wedding. My father had died earlier that year of a heart attack at age 44. No accident that I managed to find and fall in love with and marry someone a little like him, within five months.

Truth is, while we were "in love," we really didn't know each other very well. He was not very social, and I was a very outgoing person. We were very young to figure out how to live with another person. We stayed married from 1965-1970, till I was 25. Did you see the movie Mr. Holland's Opus *about a band teacher in a small town? I was like Richard Dreyfuss's wife, but during those years while he was the band teacher, I finished college and my teaching credential, taught high school in Sacramento and even finished a Master's Degree.*

What went wrong? Why did I leave? We had great sex, but that's about all. Lots of other parts of a full relationship were missing. We just weren't socially mated. He was a long-distance runner and into quiet and solitude. We never fought, but that's because we hardly ever talked about anything until it was too late. He had this weird sense of humor and sometimes made fun of me, even in public.

Pete Hanson's gifts to me were: a deep appreciation for both classical and jazz music, reading (we loved many of the same books), and of course sex as he was my first and very best (till Larry) lover.

Marriage #2—Sam Atherton, on August 29, 1979

I was 34, and we'd lived together for four years by then, restoring a 150-year-old farmhouse in upstate New York that I'd bought before I met him. I first saw him from the window of a girlfriend's house in that village, as he was lifting a beam on the house next door. When my girlfriend told me he was an architect and had just moved in to help restore that house, I ran over and introduced myself. Funny, he looked like he a huskier Pete Hanson: also blonde and balding at 25 (I was 30). We were living together in my house within a week. We had similar tastes in music and food, and friends and politics. I was working on my Ph.D while he was studying for his architect's license.

Why'd we get married after four years? We were ready to have children. I knew he'd be a great father to the two blonde haired brown-eyed boys I always knew I would have. We also wanted to have a party and let all our friends celebrate the work we'd done on the house. We weren't really religious and didn't go to church weekly, but the Episcopal priest who happened to live across the street and had a huge lawn and beautiful garden married us. We wrote the ceremony ourselves and everyone loved and still remembers it. It was one of those storybook weddings: we marched out to the beginning of Elton John's Funeral for a Friend *from his* Yellow Brick Road *album.*

We gave a rose to each of our mothers and grandmothers and thanked them for playing a part in our being there. Our vows were not the traditional "till death do us part" stuff. Rather we promised aloud together to put more "acceptance, honesty, peacefulness, respect and playfulness" into our lives. Unfortunately, these were bigger challenges than we realized at the time. We were together from 1976 to 1986.

Why'd we break up when our two children were two and four? It was time. We had more in common, and we were better socially mated than marriage #1, but there were lots of things we both didn't like about each other. In fact sometimes I thought he hated me. We spent four years in counseling on and off working on our issues. When we decided to get divorced, we said it was to give our kids a better model for a love relationship than ours. Brad, your biological father, was four, and your uncle Brian was two.

Sam Atherton's gift to me, besides the beautiful boys he was a great father to, was architecture. We went to Finland and Denmark on our honeymoon. He gave me a whole new level of appreciation for buildings in every country: a wider way of looking at the world.

I saved the best for last.

Marriage #3—Your Grandpa Larry, on May 6, 2001

We called our wedding on May 6, 2001, "The Seven Year Hitch." We held it a guesthouse on the coast of Big Sur where we'd gone the day we met at a spiritual conference in Asilomar, California. I was 49 and he was 45. I'd been single ten years, and he was divorced almost two. He had a son close in age to your father, and a stepdaughter.

Ours was the involuntary "you-know-it-from-the-first-moment" kind of love. At different periods in our lives we had been doing similar things, like living parallel lives. We'd both done a lot of psychological work on ourselves, had changed careers a few times, and were exploring our relationship with God and our spirituality. We were both attracted to one another intellectually as well as physically. He was really handsome but had dark hair and moustache and looked like a young Ernest Hemingway or Jeremy Irons, not like my ex's #1 and #2.

Our like-mindedness makes this relationship so intense and passionate, still now after 16 years. Each time I return home after being away, even this year, I get that excited feeling in my chest and we run to meet one another and hug and kiss. Once early on, someone remarked that we were joined at the hip and Larry responded, "Yes, that and the cerebral cortex!" That is part of the brain.

The gifts this man still to this day gives me (and I him) are an acceptance of one another that is as close to the unconditional love that God gives, a patience with each other's differences in timing, a tolerance for our shortcomings, a maturity that transcends the trivial, and an ability to sit down and communicate like adults when problems arise, and God knows we've been through some together!

LIFE LESSON: I call Larry my "Significant Equal." We both feel we get back from each other equal amounts, if not sometimes more, than we give. And that exchange of energy keeps on growing! And that is love personified.

LIFE: LESSON: I only wish for you both, that you learn

whatever it is you need to live alone, and then find a partner half as good, or even better, than what Larry has been for me. But I hope you find this kind of love when you are way younger than 49.

It's almost Valentine's Day; so let's hear it for love!!!
Big LOVE to you,
Grandma Pat

⬦ ⬨ ⬦

Valentine's Days Are Difficult

Sunday February 14, 2010
Dear Annie & Carter,

Happy Valentine's Day! I am so sorry that I can't be with you on this special day. A friend just sent me this e-mail, which brought tears to my eyes:

"We had our three California gran'chillun (3,6,7) sleepover last night for the three-day weekend, so we've been going gang-busters...heart-shaped PB&J's for lunch, heart-shaped crust for the choose your own fillings pizza. I conducted the customary tooth inspection (same one their dad got at their age), and have just now tucked them in after a full day."

Well I sure wish you were visiting me for the weekend. We'd have made cookies, and maybe even our own personal Valentines out of lace paper doilies and red construction paper. Or better yet, maybe they would be green. Yup, green was color of the first real Valentines, before the Hallmark card company and chocolate factories turned this into a big commercial event. It is also the color of the heart chakra (one of seven centers of power in the body).

The real Valentine's story, as I learned it, goes that a man named Valentine was jailed because he was a revolutionary (someone who has new ideas and a lot of followers) in the 14th century. He was locked up in a tower because of his radical beliefs. He sent messages to his followers scratched into chestnut leaves that he let float to the ground. Thus the color of these somewhat heart-shaped leaves was green.

It has been three years since the first Valentine's Day that I wasn't able to see you or send something. For some reason I have yet to understand, your mother decided not to pick up the phone any more when I called. Sometimes

I hate call-waiting for making her able to do that! Julie, your father's stepmother who you do still get to see, was sending you a Valentine package. Back then, she agreed to slip the DVD of March of the Penguins *into it that I had gotten for you for that Christmas, but we weren't able to visit you. You had liked* Happy Feet *that I gave you so much that penguins became a kind of symbol between you and me. Do you still have those penguin plastic glasses I gave you? Or any of the other toys?*

I have another big stuffed penguin, a really big one, waiting for you here on the landing of my staircase, where the tiger, the elephant, the lion in a denim jacket, and the two teddy bears that were Uncle Brian's are. Remember that day we played dress-up with them? You were soooo creative. That was the last day you were ever at this house. You told me you loved the tie-dye scarf I let you take home. It's probably an antique, keep it!

Well, I hope you sent and got exactly as many Valentines as you deserve. No, even more. To me that would be an infinite (unlimited, not measurable) number, because that's what love really is. Love is a feeling that when expressed creates more and more of itself.

I love you! And our connection is never broken; it's like an invisible string.

Grandma Pat

P.S. If I mailed you a book for Valentine's Day it would be The Invisible String *by Patrice Karst © 2000 DeVorss Publications*

⊡ ⊞ ⊡

From Maiden to Mother to Crone

Sunday October 15, 2012
Dear Annie,

How I wish I could see how you are growing into a young woman, a "maiden" in the three phases of women's lives: Maiden, Mother and Crone. The maiden is the stage of youthfulness, playfulness and innocence before your body announces with menstruation (your first "period" or monthly bleeding that I'm sure your mother told you about), that you could move into the next phase of "mother."

Then you get 40 years (sounds like a lot doesn't it?), of the motherhood or the creative phase in which you can birth either children and/or your best work in the world. When you stop menstruation after menopause, somewhere between 45 and 55, you get the honor of being called a "Crone." That word comes from the Greek word meaning "crowned" or "holy one" or "wise elder woman," like me at 67. It is the stage in a woman's life when she stands in her own truth and power.

I just got home from a national gathering of 200 women called *Crones Counsel* in Salt Lake City. There we attended a Red Tent Ceremony that prompted me to think of you. In ancient Hebrew times the red tent was a place women were sent when they were bleeding for ritual and rest. Some men at that time thought women were "unclean" during menstruation. The counsel built these three beautiful tents with sparkling see-through veils. Groups of younger women were invited and we elders moved with them to each tent to listen and share with one another, about the greatest tasks and challenges of each stage.

I was particularly moved at the Maiden tent when one young teenager, tears in her eyes, shared about *guys having it so much easier than girls on looks and appearance. She told us that guys take pictures of girls and post them on a website called ratingmylooks. com, and rate them from 1-10 and make often nasty comments! How awful! How horrible that must make you feel, whether you got a 9 or 10 and were chased by boys for only your looks, or a 2-3 and were laughed at!*

LIFE LESSON: Annie, I hope that you learn to believe in your own inner beauty when you look in the mirror and at your girlfriends, and not let what others say about you affect you; but I know that won't be easy.

Then I went to the Motherhood tent. A young woman of 22 with seven-month-old twins and a three-year-old at home who she loved very much, told us weeping that she was overwhelmed and didn't think she ever was "enough" for her babies! She wanted to know if we grandmother and great grandmother types had ever felt that way. We all assured her YES! And suggested ways she could ask for help when she needs it.

So Annie, I heard these Red Tent Ceremonies are being held by and for women all over the world to bring women of all ages together. I am sorry I cannot bring you to one, yet. I still hope the day will come that maybe I can.

May your journey to womanhood be a smooth and glittering one, with lots of support from your girlfriends and women elders along the way. I love you.

Invisible Grandma Pat

▢ ▣ ▢

Family Issues

Great Grandma Wilkin's Memoir-ies

January 13th 2010
Dear Carter and Annie,

I've told you about how I have always wanted to be a writer, right? Actually my mother, your great-grandmother who is still alive at 89 and living in a retirement home in New Jersey, did too. When my sisters and I were in grade school she was an English and Latin teacher. At that time in the 1950's she sent articles to magazines like American Girl *or* Ladies Home Journal. *I remember one about me learning to swim at Girl Scout camp that actually got published. She also wrote and edited a history of the town we grew up in,* This Is Clifton, *for the League of Women Voters.*

Whenever I had term papers for homework, she would help with the sentence structure and grammar. I remember vividly her tiny half-script half-print handwriting in red ink correcting my errors and making critical comments. When I was in college, and even more recently when I was writing articles for magazines (and I've had many in print), I would send her my stuff, and she would always have something to say about them, but it was usually negative. Red ink all the way. I'm sure she just wanted me to improve, but Grandma Wilkin had a hard life and often a lot of what comes out of her mouth is critical and sounds sour. She is very smart and judges people by the amount of formal schooling they've had, and the degrees after their name. (In fact she judges everything.) Lucky for me I got a Ph.D!

Over the years I've worked out some of my feelings about this in therapy. **LIFE LESSON: It isn't easy feeling that nothing you can do or write or say is "good enough." The process of getting feedback on your work**

or art from people "above you" at school or on a job is
almost always difficult but you can learn from it.

Well I am writing this today, because I had a
realization about criticism and about how people's
minds grow. About 20 years ago when Grandma Wilkin
retired to a "Leisure Village" community in New Jersey,
she took a class on writing memoirs. Those are books
that remember and capture the story of someone's life.
Last year when I visited, I found pages she'd written. She
still had them on her computer. She wrote about her
father William J. Bridges, born in 1875, and her mother
Mary Alice Whalen born in 1873, and her retarded sister
Betty born in 1923 two years after her. There were other
chapters about the house they built that I lived in when I
was a baby, as well as vacations, games they played and
the special college/high school she went to. Her writing
went all the way up to one chapter she titled "Choosing
a Husband." That was my father Jack. I wondered why
she stopped there. Theirs was a troubled relationship and
years later she blamed a lot of her problems on choosing
the wrong husband.

For Great-grandma's Christmas gift this year, I put all
the chapters in order, and edited them, never showing
her own "red ink." Larry made a cover and inserted
pictures. We made them into a book entitled Mary B.
Wilkin's Memoir-ies. We made copies for all her children
and grandchildren. I am saving one for you.

She was thrilled of course and thanked us profusely.
But my realization came when she called and said, "I re-
read them all and was surprised at how well written they
were." By that she meant the punctuation and grammar
were perfect.

As I was putting the book together, my almost
65-year-old self was surprised at the fact that there was
very little "affect," in other words there were hardly any

*feelings shown in any of the painful scenes she described.
In a story on "Games in the 1920's" she describes falling
off her roller skates with:*

*"The injury however, was not just a scraped knee. My
elbow wouldn't move. Since our doctor lived just around
the corner, my mother walked me over to Dr. McGee and
he said it was a dislocated elbow. Without even taking
me into the house, he gave one strong quick pull on the
arm and reset the elbow right on his front lawn."*

*Yikes! No description of what that felt like at all?
When my mother was thirteen, her mother died of breast
cancer! All she said about it in her memoir was:*

*"That summer I had no idea how sick my mother
was. I was just impatient for her to get better so that we
could go on our annual vacation to Boston or at least
take day trips to places where there was swimming. My
afternoons were spent across the street on the screened-
in porch of my girlfriend. We spent hours playing card
games with her mother. She taught us pinochle, flinch,
hearts and several other games.*

*On the morning of August 31, 1933, I woke to find my
father sitting on the top step of the stairs waiting for me
to wake up. He had to tell me the unbelievable news that
my mother had died. I don't remember my immediate
reaction. I was too stunned. It was too unreal that she
wouldn't be around anymore. I wouldn't be able to talk
to her again—EVER! How could this house exist without
Mother?"*

*She did go on to talk about crying at the funeral,
especially when they lowered the casket into the grave;
but reading this gave me insight into what made my
mother "shut down" and remain so critical of people and
things for the rest of her life. I became more empathic
and forgiving of her judgments of me...somewhat.*

Her comments about the writing really surprised me. Yes,

her stuff had good sentence structure and punctuation, but I had to put it in order to make it appear like a story, and the descriptions were very "this is this, and that is that, and then this happened." Good writing to me has more depth and metaphors (words that are symbols of other things) in it. Good writing makes you cry or scream with joy as you read descriptions of the characters' feelings.

LIFE LESSON: So the realization I had was twofold. First, I learned to take a different perspective or view about criticism. By not taking too personally what someone who is putting you down says, we can rise above feeling bad about not doing stuff "the right way." What people say about you often says more about them than you. That is called projection, they may be transferring feelings they have about themselves onto you.

There are many ways to do things. Just good punctuation alone is not good writing. When we look at where the person doing the "red ink" on our work (or our life for that matter) is coming from, we can take their disapproval in a different light. We might be able to shake or release it. Or perhaps we could take what works for us and forget the rest. Some people do have more expertise and things we can learn from.

Second, I realized that somehow after 65 years I have grown beyond my mother. That is huge! They say "the child becomes the father of the man," so maybe this means that I, the firstborn daughter, have grown to become in some weird way smarter or wiser (and maybe a better writer) than my mother was at this stage in her life. But oops, there I go making judgments just like she does!

Well that is enough "heady" stuff for now. I do hope you ask your mother and other grandmother and great-

*grandmother if you have one, about their memoir-ies.
You will learn a lot about what life was like almost a
hundred years ago, in the very family that contributed
the genes or the DNA to your growing 7-year-old mind
and body.*

Bye for now!
Grandma Pat (Wilkin) Hanson

Why Do Holidays Bring Out Family Dysfunction?

January 13th 2010
Dear Annie,
  Wherever you are, I'm sure your house is filled with the activities of holiday cooking. Your mom or John's mom has probably already bought a turkey, the makings for pumpkin pies, and loaves of bread to leave out overnight to get stale and then be ripped up into little pieces and cooked with onion & celery for the stuffing. We used to do that every year while watching the Macy's Parade with those big balloons on TV. You used to love to make cookies with me from scratch when you were as little as three. I wonder what part you play now in cooking Thanksgiving dinner?

  Today, however, I really want to write about the feelings I am having right now. This holiday is about being thankful for what we do have, especially now in hard times when so many people are losing their jobs and having difficulty making ends meet. I'm sure in school you got the story of the pilgrims who came to America celebrating their first harvest with a feast. But it goes beyond that. Like Christmas, the meaning of Thanksgiving has been twisted by media and commercialism to be centered on the food and not the gratitude.

  It's also a time when members of families that live far apart come together. Truth be known, for my New Jersey family and me at least, the holidays were when some of the most "dysfunctional family patterns" crept to the surface. What's dysfunctional? It's when people disagree and get mean and nasty with one another, or keep things to themselves and act weird. Of course this can be stimulated by the beer the men drink while watching football, and the things the women talk about when they are cooking (and usually cleaning up) in the kitchen.

Thanksgiving is a holiday where we're supposed to show love and tell people how we appreciate them, and on Christmas we do it with gifts of some sort.

One of the things I am really thankful for is that Larry's family never got much into the watching football and drinking beer thing. So now that there is only his mother, Larry and I do all the cooking.

Yet, all of this so far has been "window dressing" for how I'm really feeling. Brad your father will be here tomorrow. I haven't heard from him all year except Mother's Day when he always manages to call. He called even that year and a half he "went missing." In those awful days when no one knew where he was, he still called at ten minutes to midnight and said real fast "Happy Mother's Day mom, I just wanted to call. But don't ask anything about where I am or I'll hang up." I just swallowed my tongue and said I was soooo glad to hear his voice and that I loved him, always had and always will. The "bye mom" came quickly. It was a way short call.

Yesterday, as a "gift" I cleaned Grandma Kingsland's refrigerators. She has two, and the one in the garage had stains under the glass and drips of old sauces and things that an 84-year-old, 78-pound itty-bitty woman just wouldn't have the energy or time to do. I took the shelves apart and did it as a surprise when she was out. And then while we were washing dishes and everyone was home, I took some drawers of the inside refrigerator out and washed them and the shelves. I think I rearranged a few things.

Grandma was sitting at the Formica kitchen table watching the news on her 12-inch TV on the counter where she always sits, where she could see me out of the corner of her eye. Funny thing though, she's usually very bubbly and thanks everyone for everything right

*away and she said nothing to me about the refrigerators.
I know she noticed. So the next day, today, I apologized
and asked if "my gift" of cleaning had offended her, or if
she saw it as an insult to her housekeeping.*

*She admitted that she didn't like people messing with
her stuff, and that she had let it go a long time. She also
told me no one had noticed how clean everything else
was. All the crystal and glasses in a dining room cabinet,
and all the little porcelain birdies and things in the living
room were sparkling.*

*Ooops! I had mentioned it to Larry, but I didn't
immediately oooh and aaah to her.* **LIFE LESSON: Guess
I learned a lesson. No, two lessons: #1: Before you do
things you think will help someone, you should ask.
#2: Sometimes it's hard to think before you speak or
act, but take a breath and do it, it'll help. #3: When you
notice little things that need to be praised, speak up.**

*Grandma Kingsland's husband of 61 years died
less than a year ago. I think part of the reason she
was so quiet and grumpy is that she was missing him.
Sometimes it's hard for me to think before I act or speak.
Well, I'm glad I faced my discomfort the next day and we
worked it out. She was smileyer today.*

*I wish you could write back and tell me your favorite
holiday foods, or better yet what you are truly thankful
for right here, right now.*

Love and blessings, Invisible Grandma

▢ ▢ ▢

Compulsive Cleaning? OCD? Or Just Chores?

March 28th 2010
Dear Annie,

I think your mom would consider me a "clean freak." It's Sunday morning and I'm home alone. I could have been using the best time of the day for me to write, but I just spent over twenty minutes relentlessly (without stopping), scrubbing the walls of the tiny plastic shower/bathtub we have in this house with Tilex. Of course it hadn't been done in months, but I went at it with a vengeance! (an extreme or intense manner). I even took a knife to the cracks that were black and filled with mold.

One way or other I wanted to get the things that cause my allergies to make me cough OUT of this house. When I finished I put lavender cream on my hands to cover the chlorine-y smell. Then when I went to my desk. It was messy and dusty. So I threw out papers I didn't need and then dusted it with a wet rag.

*Now what I want you to know, is that although some would call what I'd just done "compulsive" or label it "obsessive compulsive disorder" (OCD), and send someone who acts like this to a doctor for drugs, I don't. I don't call fiddling around like this before I need to write procrastination either. (Remember, I told you in another letter that "pro-cras-tin-a-tion" was about putting hard things off till the last minute.) This may be my rationalization (an excuse for doing something), but I think that sometimes when we shuffle papers, or arrange our desktop, or look for magazines before doing an art project, that this is a good thing. **LIFE LESSON: Sometimes the thoughts we have in the PRE-creative procrastination period are new and turn into something good that we wouldn't have thought of before.***

Speaking of cleaning, do you get an "allowance" for doing chores around your house? Do you like things when they're clean? Do you notice?
When I was ten I used to get 10 cents an hour for babysitting my sisters then 8 and 7. All three of us had a chart that had to be checked off, that listed jobs we rotated, for which we'd get $1.50 weekly if we did them all, and did them all right.

Chore	PAT	JEAN	JANE
Wash dinner dishes			
Dry/Put Away " "			
Take garbage out			
Clean my room			
Fold Laundry			

Soooo, regardless, I hope you are having a great Sunday, and do some of the things you love; even if you have to do chores first before you get to them.
Love,
Grandma Pat

☐ ☐ ☐

Tips for Getting Along in Life
Watch Your Language

May 9, 2009
Dear Carter and Annie,

I learned the hard way from an early age that bad words can make people mad. When I was in the 5th grade I called Jackie O'Donnell a "bastard" when he took some art supplies from me and he actually hit me! We both got sent to the principal's office.

I was shocked, as I'd heard the word so often at home, I didn't know that it was a bad word! I had heard my father's language called "salty," but didn't know what that meant either. Funny, technically bastard means a boy who doesn't have a married father or mother. I guess I insulted him. Now I realize that language is full of swear words that can offend and alienate people (push them away).

LIFE LESSON: Do heed my words: if you have a strong feeling describe it; but blurting out words you know are negative because you've seen someone's reaction to them will only make them think badly of you! *I wouldn't want that to happen.*

Love,
Grandma Pat

◦ ◽ ◦

My Broken Listener

February 23, 2010
Dear Annie & Carter,
  I have a bad habit I'd like to get rid of. I interrupt people. Sometimes I get so excited about what they are saying that I butt in and say something. Or I get impatient and want to finish their sentences for them. It can drive people crazy. One of my ex-husbands accused me of having a "broken listener." He might be right. Sometimes in my excitement to comment on what people say, I do feel like I have a machine inside my head that runs wild, without brakes, and can't stop.
  When I was growing up in New Jersey our family was like that. There used to be a "LOUD" family on Saturday Night Live where everyone talked at once. It was just like that in our house. No one ever really listened to one another. We were always competing to get a word in edgewise. I developed a very loud voice because of it. That is a very hard habit to break, especially when you're in a one-on-one relationship that you want to work.
  My first husband's way of dealing with me was to withdraw and just not talk. I'd always have to be the one to start a conversation. That got old fast. Sam, your father's father, always used to "Ssshh" me all the time, even in public in front of other people. It was one of the things that pushed me to end that relationship. It was very hard at the time because your dad Brad was four, and his brother your uncle Brian, was two. Back then people told me they liked to be with each of us... separately. We were both interesting people, but together our chemistry was terrible, toxic! I'd had enough of feeling like my voice was being snuffed out. We got divorced. However, we soon found out that when you have kids, you still have to communicate about lots of things the rest of

your life. But thank goodness, it's easier from a distance.

Now eighteen years into a great relationship with Larry, I have an example of how he helps me to break my bad habit. Sometimes he just puts his hand up behind his ear as a signal that my voice is getting a little loud. Or he may signal me to come closer to whisper if we're out. Actually as we get older we're both discovering that we're a little deaf and need to talk a little loud or shout when we're in the next room. Shouting can scare some people, especially if in their family home there was a lot of anger.

Just this Saturday morning, Larry was telling me something and I interrupted. I could see he was getting frustrated, mad. So he just stopped, and waited till I was done. Then he told me nicely that when I did that, he forgets what he was going to say. He said that this was especially hard because as we age, remembering little things you just thought becomes harder and harder.

When I really want to listen to someone, it's really easy. Larry and I love the end of the day at home when we both can sit down at and ask each other how our days have gone.

I truly hope both of you have lots of friends and teachers and relatives that you can and do listen to very well. **LIFE LESSON: The older I get, the more I think other people have something important to say. I can't learn anything from them when I'm busy spouting out my reply. Listening is very important!**

So here's to the many conversations we aren't having. I only put them on paper right now. Perhaps someday somewhere we will have them before I get too old. I promise to listen. May you not have a broken listener.

Be WELL today. I love you both. And you can never say that too loud!

Grandma Pat

Thank-you's Are Important

November 21, 2011
Dear Carter and Annie,
   I'll bet the smells of pies being baked and turkey roasting is filling your homes. Instead of Thanksgiving Day I call this "Gratitude Week." I make a point of writing or calling people to thank them for things big or little they have done this year that helped me or touched my heart. I just wrote an e-mail to Great Western to tell them how good one of their tellers was when I lost my debit card. I also filled a survey out from Staples, mentioning how helpful one of the copy managers was when she matched a price she overheard me calling another store about, and saved me about $50.00! I think all year long we too often forget to do this.
   I remember how I used to make your father Brad sign thank-you notes to his grandmother for Christmas gifts even before he could write. Then he'd write his own on little cards. As he and grandma got older she'd send money on birthdays; but I'd have to bug Brad to at least call and thank her. She's not the nicest person to talk to, but what are a few minutes? Once Grandma Wilkin got so ornery about thank-you notes that if she didn't get one, she'd not send him something the following year.
   LIFE LESSON: Beyond handwritten notes and sharing our appreciations to others, most importantly we need to thank the universe, or God, or whatever force we believe is behind things, for the good in our lives. *Sometimes when things are awful and we're in a bad mood and nothing seems to be going right in our own lives, we have to pinch ourselves and find something to be glad for. Every day we have to look at our own lives, realize how lucky we are to be safe and sound and healthy, and find something to be grateful for. Today for*

me it's the sun that has just broken through a rainy day and it's 61 degrees outside in November! Today I am not in the cold Northeast, or a victim of a hurricane that flooded my house, or without heat or water. Today I am alive and well. Thank you God!

What is it this year, or this minute, that you are most thankful for?

Have fun with all the Thanksgiving festivities, and perhaps think about thanking the turkey for sacrificing its life to become your delicious dinner.

Fondly,
Grandma Pat

Go On With the Show

October 31, 2012
Dear Annie & Carter,

Halloween is my favorite holiday. I like it far better than Christmas. On Halloween you get to dress up and pretend to be anyone you want; on Christmas in my family you had to dress up and pretend too, but it was often to spend time and give gifts to relatives you didn't like just because you were supposed to. Enough said, more on that in another letter.

Last night I was supposed to be on stage at Monterey's Golden State Theatre as part of A Vaudeville Show *and be the narrator in a 15-minute pantomime play. In it three actors were to walk through this really macabre (meaning ghastly or gruesome) script that had dead bodies and a creepy mortician in it. I was all dressed up in black bolero hat, boots, and black* SIX FEET UNDER *t-shirt from the HBO TV series about a funeral home that I loved. On front it had a big face being lip-sticked by an undertaker.*

But even though we rehearsed the play Sunday for two hours, two of the four actors called in "sick" at the last minute and the director cancelled it. I was soooo disappointed, as I'd worked hard re-typing my script so the actors could see their cues. I'm not a singer by a long shot, and yet I was ready to sing "Swing Low Sweet Chariot" from the stage and get the audience to join in!

Well, there's a lesson in this somewhere. The director was a little pushed out of shape when I suggested I'd bring some votive candles and a TV tray (that were in her script) and changed a few of her words to make them shorter. Like "I have" to I've. At one point she got angry with me for having "too much enthusiasm." This has happened to me before. To keep things like this from happening over and over **LIFE LESSON: I learned to really** *listen to what people (especially bosses on jobs) are telling me, and then sometimes to just swallow and say nothing and "let go."* However that's not too easy for me.

The actors that called in hadn't really been on a stage before. I think they weren't so much "sick" as afraid they'd screw up. This kind of stage-fright before a performance happens to everyone. I'm sure you've felt it before sports games or things you have to do in school before the entire class. **LIFE LESSON: Whatever you do, you "practice, practice, practice," and don't quit at the last minute. Do the best you can, knowing it's only a show. In the scheme of things one night is really nothing.**

So I stayed home and watched a funny movie instead.

May you have many treats and not too many tricks on all your Halloweens.

Your Invisible Grandma Pat

◻ ◻ ◻

Peace and Politics
Arlington West: Veterans for Peace Memorial

Monday August 26, 2008
Dear Annie & Carter,
   Yesterday morning I took a walk on the boulevard, Carrillo Ave, in Santa Barbara. It is at the end of their main shopping street where a wharf begins that has shops and restaurants. Your father and his brother Uncle Brian, who is now a soldier, used to love to go fishing from that pier every summer.

   Much to my surprise today, on the beach next to the wharf was a flat space in the sand with 3,000+ tiny little crosses with names on them. Some had pictures and flowers next to them. They represented the 4,146 U.S. soldiers, both men and women, that have died so far serving our country in the Iraq war since 2004. 30,324 more soldiers have been wounded, and an estimated 650,000 Iraqis have died.

   This memorial called Arlington West was built by a group of retired soldiers called "Veterans for Peace." It was designed like the big cemetery in Virginia for people killed in World War I and World War II that has the famous statue of five soldiers holding up a flag on Iwo Jima in Japan.

   It was very very VERY sad for me to walk past all the reminders of the not so little sacrifices (look up that word) that each of these soldiers made for our country in a war. Your uncle went to Iraq and was one of the lucky ones who came back whole after his six-month tour of duty. He is an officer and a special type of soldier called a Navy Seal. Very few men make it through the training to be this type of warrior. He chose to go to a military academy for college, and now calls himself one of the "alpha males" of the military. That word is used for things that are the strongest and brightest which he is. I like seeing the yellow ribbons on cars that say "Support Our Troops." All people in the armed services need to know we care about their lives.

However, I personally do not like this war, nor do the Veterans for Peace. I think the Iraq war is not doing much to stop terrorism (talk about that word on September 11th with your folks). I think it is costing the government lots of money that would be better spent on schools for young people like you, and roads, and health care for all Americans. It costs two billion dollars a week (!) Try putting those numbers with all their zeroes on paper, and ask your parents to look up how much is spent on schools in comparison.

What have you been taught about war at home or in school? I will look forward to hearing from you about this when the time comes. And I know your Uncle Brian would love to meet you when he is not sent around the world somewhere. He is home now and won't be deployed (another word for sent to a war zone) until March 2009.

Let's pray and send blessings to everyone involved in making decisions about this and other wars.

I love you.

Grandma Pat

The Election: A Not Impossible Dream

November 1, 2008
Dear Annie & Carter,

Last night on Halloween Larry and I took a break from the video we are making, turned the lights off and went to a movie. We didn't want to stay home and give more candy to trick or treater kids than they need.

Know why? Because this very important election for President has been consuming all our energy and taking our time. Are they talking about it in your school? It is soooo important that people vote!

Unfortunately in 2004 only 55% of people in the U.S. who were eligible (old enough and citizens) to vote did so. In 2000 only 51% did. To my shock and dismay, somehow they elected a man who will go down in history as the WORST president ever! President George W. Bush really got only 30% of eligible voters! Don't get me started! His administration was the worst ever. Democrat Bill Clinton left the budget in the black, meaning no deficit and debt, and now 8 years later the United States is 9.6 trillion dollars in debt, the economy tanked because of corrupt greedy bankers, and we've killed over 4,400 US soldiers in a war that Republicans led us into for all the wrong reasons.

If you were around I'm sure you'd hear lots of political talk, most of it loud, these days. What I really wanted to write you about is what I am doing to make sure people vote. Two things: I am working with a group called "moveon.org" and making phone calls to voters in "swing states," (that means states with lots of electoral votes that could make or break the election), to make sure they vote. Moveon has lists of registered voters that are undecided and/or voted independent or Republican last time.

Also, we are distributing to every state Democrat organizing office, and other big media groups, a new recording of a song "The Impossible Dream" by one of our favorite singers, a big black blues singer named Sister Monica Parker. It is very famous, from a Broadway Play called "Man of La Mancha." If we were somewhere this musical was in a theatre, I'm sure I would've taken you by now. It is the inspiring story of Don Quixote, a kind of loner, but brilliant guy back in the 17th century who went on a quest no one believed in. Much to many people's surprise he actually did accomplish his dream because he believed in it and himself.

Sister Monica's new version of this epic song weaves the voices of both Dr. Martin Luther King (surely they've taught you about him in school: there's a holiday for him every January) and President-elect Barack Obama, in between her words of the song. Larry videotaped and edited a You-Tube version. Look at it. The woman on the right side of the screen is "signing" the words for deaf people. Isn't that terrific? We were only able to get it up a day before the election and it has gotten 30,000 hits already.

So, regardless of how your mom and dad vote, know that your Invisible Grandmother has great hope for change for America, when (not if) Barack Obama is elected the winner and becomes the first black president of the YOU-knighted-states!

LIFE LESSON: May you dream many "impossible dreams," and have them come true!

Love,
Your political Grandma Pat

□ ▣ □

The Election Is Over. Wear Purple!

November 1, 2008
Dear Annie & Carter:
   Where I live, people climb up on the sand dunes on Route One and write messages in iceplant every day. Usually it's love notes, or Happy Birthday Joe type of things; but yesterday's read: BAROCK THE VOTE! And Thank goodness he did!! I make no bones about being a lifelong Democrat: the people's party, in comparison to Republicans who seem more to be about business and money.
   I can now put away my Women for Obama button away with my flashing red, white and blue beads and pin that reads Barack Obama 2008. I wonder if my mother still has the little rhinestone pin I had back in 1952 and 1956 that read Adlai for Adlai Stevenson. He was a very smart man (a Democrat) who ran twice against a very popular military golfer type who won: Dwight D. Eisenhower. His button read just I Like Ike.
   All week I wore an Obama T-shirt I got for making phone calls for him in 2008. On the front it says: "ONE VOICE CAN CHANGE THE WORLD." On the back it goes on to read:
   THE POWER OF ONE VOICE
   IF ONE VOICE CAN CHANGE
   A ROOM
   THEN IT CAN CHANGE
   A CITY
   IF IT CAN CHANGE A CITY
   THEN IT CAN CHANGE
   A STATE
   IF IT CAN CHANGE A STATE
   THEN IT CAN CHANGE
   A NATION

IF IT CAN CHANGE A NATION
THEN IT CAN CHANGE
THE WORLD

That's may be a pretty hard concept for you to fully understand right now; but really **LIFE LESSON: every person young or old, small or large, dark-skinned or white, gay or straight, deserves to be heard, and yes, to vote for people who will have the power to make decisions that will affect their lives.**

Elections are a lot different now. Way TOO different if you ask me. Back then I walked neighborhoods knocking on doors with my father, and explaining the different ideas to people. Today I'm glad this election is over, because far too much money was spent on often nasty and bitter television ads, many of them lies. The most money ever spent on an election, today's Washington Post said. TWO BILLION DOLLARS: $2,000,000,000 .... I don't even know if I got the zeroes right! That's a disgrace ... imagine what good that kind of money could do if it were spent on your schools, on health, welfare, roads and even emergency disaster relief.

I guess you were sleeping by the time our president gave another of his rousing speeches. The theme was about working together. I think Barack's line that will go down in history like John F. Kennedy's "Ask not what your country can do for you, but what you can do for your country" did. Our second term president said "America's never been about what can be done for us. It's about what can be done by us together..." He ended with reminding us "We remain more than a collection of red states and blue states. We are and forever will be the United States of America."

LIFE LESSON: Carter and Annie, we are so lucky to live in this country! I think we should all wear purple tomorrow to show the beautiful color that results when red and blue are mixed. Just think of all the good things that could happen if we set aside our differences and worked together for the common good!

I hope I am around to imagine or maybe even witness your growth, like we saw the President's daughters Sasha and Malia on stage with him this year and four years ago. I am encouraged that might actually happen by something President Obama said about hope: "I have always believed that hope is that stubborn thing inside us that insists, despite all the evidence to the contrary, that something better awaits us so long as we have the courage to keep reaching, to keep working, to keep fighting."

Just think, perhaps in 2016 or 2020 We'll celebrate the election of the first woman president!

LIFE LESSON: Pay attention in school, it's important.

I love you. Grandma Pat

◻ ▣ ◻

Church, God and Spirituality
Gentle with Myself

Sunday September 20, 2009
Dear Annie & Carter:
I thought of you a lot today, especially when the children came in to sit on the stage at the bottom of the gospel choir in our "rockin church," Inner Light Ministries in Santa Cruz. It made me sad to have to imagine that it was your blonde hair and pony tail I saw from behind, among the dozen or so children who left the sanctuary, (holy place or building), after the two songs to have "their own Funday experience." I wanted you to be there and wondered what you would think of all this.

Even before the children arrived there were tears in my eyes when the entire congregation (big word for all people at the service) were singing a tune over and over again to these words that were projected on a big screen above the stage:

I will be gentle with myself
I will be gentle with myself
I will hold myself like a newborn baby child

Annie, I remember the first time I held you when you were a month old, back in Las Vegas almost seven years ago. You were so beautiful, and still are of course. But there is something about holding babies, especially someone else's baby, that makes me afraid, sort of scared, and tells me to be overly careful with them because they seem so fragile. (Fragile? It means delicate ... not strong enough to withstand severe stresses. But I believe that deep down inside, all of us have a place where we are safe and strong and that is our soul.

Babies also make me think of all the wonderful (and sometimes awful) possibilities for their lives that they have wrapped up in that amazing tiny brain and body. It will grow and grow and grow. Its capacity is infinite. (Infinite? It means limitless, endless, immeasurable! WOW! More on that in another letter)

Do you hold your new baby sister? How does that make you feel? Do you have to help with your other sister who is now probably three? Do you love her? Sometimes does she make you mad? What a big beautiful family your mom is building.

The song also reminded me how scared I was to hold your brother Carter when I first saw him. He is now nine (!) Your biological father never got to be with him at all, he moved to California before he was born. Like your mother, Lily his mom raised him by herself till she met and married John and had two more babies: one boy now 5 and this year a baby girl. Back when I met him in 2001 there was something about the way I was becoming a grandmother that wasn't the way it's supposed to be. Something made me cry for days before I could hold Carter. I've seen him about once a year since then, and send him books every birthday and Christmas. He has lots of grandparents and step-grandparents and knows he's been adopted, but just calls me Pat. I guess to him I am a "partially visible" grandparent instead of an invisible one. I can't even send you books or Valentine's Day cards. But I am saving all these letters for you.

I love you.

Grandma Pat

◽ ◾ ◽

A Baby Blessing

Sunday, May 20, 2010
Dear Annie and Carter:
This is another letter I'm writing while weeping. I am watching our church service at Inner Light Ministries in Santa Cruz live streamed on the internet (www.innerlightministrieslive.com) It is Children's Sunday. Whether I'm there or not, each time I see the children I think of you both and wish I could bring you here every week. About 20 kids from 4 to 14 just sang this song waving beautiful scarves from the stage:

> I wish you joy … in all things you do
> I wish you love … in all things you do
> I wish you fun … in all things you do
> I wish you hope that never ends
> But most of all I wish you joy!

Then like adults do other Sundays, one or two of the children read the affirmations and led the prayers. Reverend Deborah's sermon was spoken especially to the kids. It was terrific. The theme for the month was "Bounty," meaning a reward or abundant (lots of) supply of something. The kids picked the topic "Bountiful Play."
At the end there was a baby blessing. In other churches they are called baptisms or christenings. It's when ministers or priests welcome children to the world. Your father Brad and Uncle Brian were baptized in an Episcopal church. I took them to many kinds of churches when they were school age. I've seen many baby ceremonies, but Reverend Deborah's ceremony is my favorite.
She has the parents, and all the people they name as extended family who promise to help take care of the baby, come up on the stage. She does not appoint "godfathers" or "godmothers," but engages all the

*parents and helpers, as well as everyone in the church in
making a pledge to help children by not forgetting to use
these three sentences:*

> **LIFE LESSON:**
> **Yes you can.**
> **I believe in you.**
> **I am never ever giving up on you.**

*What a way to welcome children into the world.
This makes me cry because I don't even know if your
parents bring you to church at all, or if they have had you
blessed in any way. Please understand that silently, I am
imagining/visioning a ritual like this for you. I said both
your names before that pledge and with the audience
said the sentences aloud, three times.*

*There were times it was very difficult for me to keep
those pledges, with both of my children, as well as Larry's
son… but we kept doing it, and things have improved. I'm
sure our prayers, which at times are all you can do when
your kids get to be adults, helped.*

*I love you both. Blessing upon you … from any and all
denominations.*

Grandma Pat

February 22nd, Twenty-ten Love Train!

Dear Annie & Carter,

Today I watched my wonderful husband, your Grandpa Larry, sing in the 85-person gospel choir at our church. It is streamed live on computer and because it was raining I stayed home. I could see the children sitting on the floor in front of the choir for the songs, and watched them leave for their own FunDay school once the sermon began. It was still very sad for me, thinking how much I'd like you to be there someday.

The songs they chose this week were about February's theme LOVE of course. The first one was 'Even in the Midst' and it brought tears to my eyes, again. I've heard them sing it before. The words go like this:

Please … trust that I …am with you …always …
Sharing …with you …stormy nights …sunny days.
Be still and know … that where-ever you go-oh
Even in the midst … I hear you …. I know you … I'm
    LOVing … you-ooh.

If I could mail you a CD of the service and the songs, I would. **LIFE LESSON: Basically, here's what I get about spirituality now: the "I" in the words to many songs can mean God. It means that no matter how alone you feel, or how difficult times may be, that some ONE is watching over you.** *The words of the chorus go on… even closer than breath; nearer than your mind… even closer than breath; nearer than your mind.*

Wow. To know inside that you have a spiritual guardian there for you! I sure wish I'd learned that earlier. It wasn't till I was about 45, and I can remember exactly when it happened like a light went on in my head. I really realized that if you substituted the word "God" for "him" or "her" or "I" in love songs, that they were about God missing you when you went away, or God taking care of you. They were not about finding Mr. or Ms. Right to make your life better.

I once gave a speech in a Unitarian Church in Sacramento in 1970, the year my master's thesis was a TV series on Sexuality in the Seventies. *I opened it with the song that Mary Magdalene in the Bible sings "I Don't Know How to Love Him" from the play* Jesus Christ SuperStar. *Back then I thought it was about the gulf between men and women in understanding each other. In fact I don't even think I "got it" in my 20's what that song was really about.*

The second song they sang today was "Love One Another" (by Luciane Clark Fox), once made popular by Gladys Knight, an African-American singer I love. Its basic message is:

As I have loved you, Love one another, This new commandment, Love one another, By this shall all know, Ye are my disciples, If ye have love One to A-noth-er!

The minister went on to tell everyone that these words were from the Bible, John:13, and that before Christ died on the cross, he said them. "As I have loved you, love one another." He said it was his most important message: that connection between people is what's most important, not fighting (or wars). The preacher went on to ask everyone to stand and hold their own hands and say "I love my hands," and then their arms "I love my arms,'"and so on. He asked us "What did you do today to show yourself that you love you?" Can you answer that question Annie or Carter? The old clichés (buzzwords) about loving yourself first are true.

I wonder if you have any idea of God or a higher power. I went to Sunday school in the Catholic church when I was your age, and in 1952 had a "First

Communion" ceremony in this cool white dress when
I was your age. But all I remember was memorizing a
bunch of words and getting tested on them. I knew when
we lit candles and prayed, something good was supposed
to happen, but then I went on with my life at the time
and forgot all about it. Now, spirituality (how we make
sense of the world and give life meaning) means a lot to
me. I think that gets deeper and deeper as we get older.

The last song was "Love Train." I'm sure you've heard
it. I think Smokey Robinson and the Miracles first made
it popular--years ago. For the chorus, Larry and two
other men in the choir came up front and did a doo-wop
number. "People All Over the World, Join Hands, Start a
Love Train, Love Train."

I sure wish you could've been there to dance and "rock
out" as they call it. It makes church fun; quite different
from how I remember it in my early days.

Love be with you my little ones,
Grandma Pat

⬚ ⬚ ⬚

Easter as Resurrection Day

Sunday, May 20, 2010
Dear Annie and Carter,
    Yesterday was Easter, and of course my eyes teared up again as I watched the children file into church. Not too many people had on Easter bonnets as I did. But as that tune of a very old song went came to mind "... with all the frills upon it ... dah-dah-duh-do-to ... as we walk down the Av-e-nue, Fifth Av-e-nue ... in the Easter ... Pah-rade." I remembered what a huge annual holiday that was when I was your age. Every year my mother used to sew three matching Easter outfits for me and my sisters and somewhere she found us matching hats.
    Of course, the Easter bunny always came, leaving huge baskets of marshmallow chickadees, jellybeans and chocolate bunnies. He (never she) had hidden all kinds of eggs that we had spent hours dyeing and decorating the weeks before. It was great fun, as was the family meal with cousins and aunts and uncles: usually ham and scalloped potatoes.
    We knew that this holiday was about a famous figure named Jesus Christ, who had been hung on a huge cross to die the Friday before, and somehow mysteriously arose alive three days later from behind a rock that blocked a cave on Easter morning; but I didn't really "get it" back then.
    Today I was just sad that I have absolutely no idea if either of you know the true meaning of Easter, or even have an idea what God is. Of course I want you to have the fun of the Easter egg hunts, and all the candy and ham and yams you like; but deep down I wonder if you are being raised with any sense of spirituality or religion at all. I guess I will have to just imagine that you are, and hope that someday you will come to understand the

powerful force that underlies the meaning of life.

In my chosen "new thought" religion, my minister prefers to call Easter "Resurrection Day." Our now world-famous choir that went to Carnegie Hall belted out a song "Resurrect me lord … Heal me of my old ways, oh lord, Resurrect me, lord… heal me of my own ways."

Then our minister went on to give us a new take on fundamental Christianity. She asked us to think of Easter as a time of renewal, a time not only when one widely followed healer died for our sins to save us. She sees it as more of a time when we are reminded of that Christ presence within us, and we "die" (release our old habits that are keeping us from being all that we can be). Reverend Deborah told her audience of 500+ and hundreds of others that watched it live on the internet, that the Easter story is a reminder that this spirit, the one that some call Jesus Christ, cannot be killed. It's within all of us anyway, just waiting for its wonders to be revealed!

Annie and Carter, this is all too complex for me to explain to you right now, this way, in letters. Please just know this Invisible Grandma is wishing she could be there with you year after year for celebrations of this kind. I send you unseen, all the Love and guidance you will need as you grow up. I hope you don't develop too many bad habits in need of resurrection, and I welcome following your own paths to truth as you begin to understand and practice whatever religion you may choose (or not).

Yes, I love you. And yes, I believe there is a God that loves you too!

Happy Easter! And Happy Resurrection Day!

Love,

Invisible Grandma Pat

Aging, Dying and Death
Gettin' Old

February 16, 2011
Dear Annie & Carter,
    Tonight I'm teaching a class on "Aging Positively," in other words "Getting OLD!" I wonder what "old" means to you? Food in the refrigerator that's gotten moldy? Bigger kids who are teenagers? People over 30? Or 60? Or as I now see it, over 90!?
    I used to think it was cute when Willard Scott on the "Today" show inserted pictures, usually of a woman, on a Smucker's jelly jar, and announced her 99th or 102nd birthday. Guess what? I don't any more.
    I turn si ... six ...sixty-five on my birthday March 1ˢᵗ. Every day I get reminded of how long a life that's been. When I go to the gym and set the time I want on the treadmill, and have to enter my age, I have to hold the button down till the digital numbers climb up from 35 to 65! When I fill out a form on the computer and it asks what year I was born, I have to scroll down from 2010 through 1990s, 1980s and so on, back past the 1950s to 1945! Yikes, those few seconds seem like a long long time.
    Almost every day in the mail I get envelopes with advertisements on the outside with things like a picture of a woman looking up at a cloud raining down on her that says "Turning 65 and worried about it?" or from Physician's Mutual with "Who inherits your debts if something happens to you?" Or from something called The Trident Society with an ad "Think Outside the Box: Free Prepaid Cremation!" And the television commercials about all the prescription drugs and their side effects. Eeks, it gets to be too much "in your face." The women's magazines that have all the ads for "anti-aging" creams

and pills make me crazy. People injecting Botox, which is actually poison, into their skin to keep them from looking "older" ... Forgettaboutit!

So Annie, as you turn 8 and want to be 13, or Carter you turn 10 but want to be 16 so you can get a driver's license, or 21 to legally drink, **LIFE LESSON: Like where you're at. Remember to accept the truth of your age and fill each minute with love and fun.**

I sure wish I could be in more memories of your minutes.!

Grandma Pat

Saying Good-Bye

November 5, 2009 4:00 p.m.
Dear Annie & Carter:
    I am about to do something that isn't easy. I am
about to visit my 75-year-old friend Robert, who is
homebound (meaning he hasn't been outside his tiny
apartment for over a year). He's had a heart attack
and has several diseases, like emphysema, that make it
difficult to breathe. Oxygen runs into little tubes in his
nose 24/7 from a tank near his bed. He is very thin and
frail (meaning his bones are weak). He eats food like
scrambled eggs and grilled cheese, but mainly drinks little
cans of a milkshake-like thing called ENSURE. A home
health aide comes in every day to help bathe him in bed. I
do his shopping and have helped take care of him for two
years.
    He is now under hospice care, which means he is taken
care of at home by a special team of nurses and doctors
and aides. They come to him every day to check on him
and give him medicine for his pain. He also gets spiritual
counseling. Yes, it means he is dying. And yesterday his
daughter called me to ask if I'd visit and "say good-bye."
The nurses told her that the end is close. So I am going
over there right now. I'm a little nervous, but all people
have to die someday, and I just hope his is a peaceful
passage.
    Robert had a business once that took him all over the
world. His favorite place was Egypt, and he is an expert
on numerology or what numbers mean. He watches the
History Channel with no sound on, just the words on the
screen, all day.
    I remember when I was little a lot of my mother's
aunts and uncles died in their 80's. When something
bad happened to them, or anyone, she'd have us light a

candle in church and pray for a speedy recovery (meaning they get better) or a happy death. Today they call wishes like this for a "graceful passage."

Someday we can talk about what may lie beyond life on this earth. Different religions and different cultures believe in many different possibilities. But one thing for sure is, when that person is gone, their not being around often makes people feel sad. **LIFE LESSON: Grieving a loss like that, especially if it is something like a pet turtle or puppy that didn't make it, is important. If we keep our feelings in, someday they may pop out where and when we least expect it.**

If Robert is awake I am going to tell him how much he has taught me about how to "chill," and "hang loose" as he used to say to me. And I'll remind him how much fun it was when I used to drive him to Santa Cruz for his medicine or doctor's appointments. We would stop at the beach and have lunch looking at it from the car. Wish me luck.

Love,
Grandma Pat

P.S. November 5, 2009 9:00 pm
So that wasn't so bad. Robert was thinner than last I saw him two weeks ago, and he was saying some things that didn't make sense, but he recognized me and took my hand. Actually he looked sort of serene, calm. One of his aides came in while I was there. She was beautiful, dark-skinned and had a white flower in her dark hair that was piled up on her head. Her name was Maile. She was named after a flower in Hawaii where Robert once lived. She mentioned she liked to sing. Robert wanted her to sing "Bali Hai." It's from the musical South Pacific about a soldier in WWII who falls in love with a Polynesian woman but can't marry her. But Maile didn't know the

song. *Before I visit next I will try to find that song on the Internet, put it on my iPod and bring it for him to hear, and maybe even leave it on CD so next visit Maile can sing it to him.*

LIFE LESSON: Saying good-bye didn't have to happen yet. And good-bye isn't necessarily a bad thing. Stay tuned.

Love,
Grandma Pat

▸ ▫ ▸

Death

November 9, 2009
Dear Annie and Carter,

Robert died Sunday morning. His daughter Gail and one of his best friends from his Navy days 40 years ago were staying in the next room. Just Saturday night they were talking with him about a big sign he'd made years ago when he'd been selling memorabilia products from World War II. So they put it up over his bed.

It said GOOD LUCK in big black letters and had a circle between the GOOD and the LUCK with spokes like a wheel in it. The sign was made on oilcloth and was about 7 feet across and 3 feet down. Robert had told us it represented the wheel of "dharma." I just looked up dharma. It means "phenomenon" or an extraordinary event! In Buddhism it means the way a person lives and works in this world, on a path toward dharma yukam or nirvana. All these words literally mean to let go from suffering. They all involve the cycle of death and rebirth or reincarnation. Wow!

Don't you think it amazing they put that sign up the night before he died? The last conversation they had with him was about the sign! Gail said she got up really early and heard Robert's breathing and it sounded noisy and rattley. He sat bolt upright in bed, and she asked him if he needed anything. He said "no," but shouted to her, "Gail, go to your room." She told me he sounded like when she was a little girl. Then he lay back down with his head way back and began breathing a little more normally.

They went out for coffee and when they came back they noticed Robert wasn't breathing at all. His spirit had left his body. He'd died. Gail said it was exactly 8:08 a.m. on November 8th. Robert was very into numerology. We'll *have to look up that combination of numbers another time.*

Gail did a lot of crying, of course, but she managed to find a Buddhist temple in Carmel, and by 1:30 in the afternoon I arrived just in time to witness a ceremony. Two Buddhist monks with shaven heads wearing robes were reading final prayers and chanting for him in a language I couldn't understand. Robert's other daughter, her husband, and Robert's 9-year-old grandson were there.

Sometimes the words sounded like "oh ma nay pa pa cay ya" ... I won't try to describe them. But it was really beautiful and peaceful. People were sad but not in pain, sad in a happy kind of way.

His daughter Gwyn sat on the bed holding his hand, and even nine-year old Konner came up and held the other hand for a little while. I had never touched a dead body before. The skin was yellowish. It just felt very thin and a little waxy. I went up and held his hand and mentally thanked him for all he'd taught me. I told him I was sorry I never got to play "Bali Hai" for him, but perhaps we'll play it at whatever other kind of funeral the family decides to do.

There are a lot of other things about funerals and taking care of what to do. I just wanted you to know about the special, I'd call them "spiritual non-accidents" that happened around and before Robert's spirit left his body and "made his transition." In my religion, that means left this earth for some other universe.

What have you been told about what happens when people die? I hope you haven't been taught to be afraid of talking about it. Have you gone to any funerals? Konner actually went to one for one of his friends who was killed in a car accident. That was terribly sudden and really sad for everyone, especially his parents.

At least Robert had lived a full life and people were ready for this to happen. My prayer for you is that you live a full life, and maybe, just maybe I will get to see you and actually know you before I leave this planet. I love you both, whether I can show it or not.

Love, Grandma Pat

A Military Funeral

Tuesday, November 17, 2009
Dear Annie & Carter,
Yesterday Robert was buried at a military cemetery in Santa Nella, California. It was a beautiful day as we drove the hour-and-a-half trip from Monterey over Pacheco Pass with bright sunlight on the rolling mountains, and wisps of fog lifting off the reservoir on Route 152. That road reminded me of Annie. I used to take it when I came every month to see her. I actually cried a little about that, more than for Robert's burial. It was time for him to go, and I wasn't that close to him. Yet I still yearn to be closer to you.

We arrived at the cemetery just in time to line up our cars and drive behind a big black Cadillac hearse (big station wagon used in funerals) to the burial site. Robert's son and son-in-law helped two other soldiers lift the flag-draped coffin out of the van onto a rolling cart.

Five retired veterans stood at attention holding rifles behind the flag-draped casket that held Robert's remains. Although I am not a minister, the family asked me to open the military service with a prayer. I put on a black graduation robe to read from Marianne Williamson's book of prayers called Illuminata.

Afterwards, everyone said I spoke very well, as if I had been leading prayer for years. I guess I have, but not in any official manner. After my reading, a chaplain in uniform took over the ceremony. He talked about the dedication to our country that all soldiers pledge, and thanked Robert and all of the men and women who serve our country in the military. Then they shot off three loud rifles in salute to Robert. I cried then, thinking of your uncle who just came back from Afghanistan. I wept for all the soldiers that hadn't come back from there and Iraq, and gave their lives for these two most recent wars. Wars that I don't understand.

Then they played Taps over the speaker system. I remember first hearing Taps at Girl Scout camp when I was nine. Each night all the campers would circle the flagpole, and they'd take down and fold the flag while a bugle played the melody and sometimes we'd sing the words:

> "Day is done,
> Gone the sun,
> From the hills,
> From the lakes,
> From the sky,
> All is well,
> Safely rest,
> God is nigh."

It was a beautiful way to mark Robert's passing. Have you been to any funerals yet? If and when you do, I hope you will not be scared and know just what to say to the people who have lost someone. They just need to know you understand. Well, that's a lot on a big subject. Enough for now.

I love you. Grandma Pat

HEALING

Separation: A Most Difficult Challenge

This last chapter covers the steps I undertook, to handle separation. Clearly to heal anything, sharing your story and your feelings about it is very important. I am grateful that I was able to have many therapy sessions, and for the many close friends I confided in, rather than keep it in. We do the work of healing because we don't want the ghosts of past ways of thinking to haunt us into the future. Even if we can only imagine the spirit of someone gone to us, we can learn to heal the wounds from these circumstances.

Erich Fromm, Abraham Maslow, and many noted psychologists report that the pain of separation is at the top of the list. The minister of the new thought church I attend tells us, "All that needs to be healed is our sense of separation." She means our separation from God, but when it comes right down to it, "getting" that is a lifelong process. As in Patricia Karst's bestselling children's book "The Invisible String," we all need to remember the "invisible string," not just of DNA but hopefully love, that connects each of us with our foremothers and forefathers.

My father died when I was nineteen. It took me till I was 25 and on an analyst's couch to fully feel and release the grief from his passing. In the early 80's I lost two close friends to AIDS, one of them the godfather of my firstborn son, Brad. I used to teach a course on Death and Dying in the Health Education Department at Chico State. I've been a Hospice Bereavement Volunteer for five years. Yet nothing prepared me for the pain and the grief that I felt when I first realized that my son's drug abuse had led to my being kept from seeing my granddaughter for an undetermined amount of time, perhaps forever. Everyone says that time heals, but when you're facing an immediate crisis, those words are not very comforting. This book has been five years in the writing, and it has been seven years since I've seen Annie. Whenever I see a young girl her age, or something else reminds me of our separation, in spite of the healing work I've done, there is still a scar on my heart that will never go away.

The Only Way Out Is Through

The first step in getting through and over anything is becoming fully aware of what is going on. As you've seen in my SNS letters, when I first confronted the reality of my situation, I was unable to keep my mind off anything but worst-case scenarios for my son's future. Dreams were tortuous. I went over and over little things, reviewing in self-deprecating ways what I may have done too much or too little of in my son's upbringing. Angry and even vengeful thoughts about who or what appeared to be blocking me arose. Fantasies of his doing harmful things bubbled up.

"Don't go there," everyone told me but that didn't help. To stop worst-case scenarios on your mind screen, they told me, "Focus on the next best thought, look for something beautiful around you." This worked in little spurts.

I kept busy with my work in the world, and searched my bag of spiritual self-help books for months. Charlotte Kasl's *Finding Joy: 101 Steps to Free Your Spirit* and *Dance with Life* helped me rise above the drama of self-absorption in my own little predicament, and see it in perspective as a "cosmic blink in time." In spite of how serious my problems felt, the earth still turns on its axis, the sun rises, stars come out and life goes on.

Ann Lamott says there are two kinds of prayer: "Help" and "Than You." I prayed every day. Sometimes when things are out of your control, turning it over to whatever higher power you believe in is the only thing you can do. At one point, every morning for 21 days, I put headphones on and listened to a twenty-minute guided visualization from The Kabbalah Centre's *Power of Kabbalah CD Set* by Michael Moskowitz. It had me imagine a split screen where I could put on one side images of where Brad was at the time, but on the other, with light from "the creator" or whatever god source I could imagine; I was to see my son thriving, my grandchildren growing up healthy and sound, my wisdom imparted to them. Eventually this helped me come to accept what was going on and begin to hold hope for a positive outcome. Each little step towards healing helped me avoid depression and moved me in the direction of getting well.

What a Great Grandparent You Would Be!

When I realized that my phone calls requesting visits to Annie were deliberately not being answered, and I started to fully grasp that I was being denied access to her, I was disappointed, shocked and then pissed. When I finally "got it" that I was being kept from participating in the life of a four-year-old I'd seen regularly since she was born, my first reaction was to get angry and self-righteous.

As I started to "feel my feelings," rather than go crazy and take them out on something or somebody else, I wrote in a journal about them. I shouted out all the good things my grandbabies would miss out on. It was an ego-centered diatribe about what they would never get by not having such a cool grandmother as me.

Bruised ego aside, I discovered that making a list of what my grandkids would miss helped me handle my feelings at the time. Here's my list:

- An intelligent presence, mine! One that can intuit a way to ask kids questions and support their growth, without having to be the direct disciplinarian;
- Lessons in cooking, cleaning, organizing, playing, and living life fully;
- Trips to places they might never have gone: Washington, D.C., New York City, Monterey, California, even across the ocean;
- Financial help with college costs (God knows what that'll be in 2019!);
- Widened perspective on gender roles, history, dress, love, movies and politics.

- Exposure to many spiritual perspectives: all the different ways "god" is in ours and other cultures; and
- Help at critical passages like menstruation, marriage, menopause, dying, death.

It might be useful for you to write a list of all the tangible and intangible experiences your grandchildren may not get, should the worst case scenario happen and you never see them again. However take a positive stance. Feel free to brag, pat yourself on the back. Get imaginative. Don't let restrictions on money limit you. List your "grandma gifts" as if in the best-case scenario, they could happen.

Read your list to yourself out loud, proudly. Observe how you felt as you did this. Did you feel different at all? Did it lighten your mood or darken it? Did you feel any better or worse? Did it bring up anger? Did anger, sadness, or joy come up? But most importantly, did you get any insight into your own goodness and greatness? Hang on to that. This is the grandparenting vibration we want to send to all future generations.

Find Something to be Grateful For

As I've grown older I have developed a widened perspective on all of my life's experiences. Many of my worst turning points turned out to be "cosmic triggers" for something better. Gratitude has become an essential part of my daily life. One morning when I was mired in confusion as to why at this was happening to me, the daily meditation I read every morning (no accident) was titled: "Don't Focus on the Missing." It was spot on:

*When we focus on what we are missing, we are
focusing on lack, loneliness, longing and loss of some kind.
The energy of that focus is really poisonous, diminishes
our relationships, makes us sad, and generally brings more
unhappy experiences to us.*

I discovered that whenever I feel myself missing my family, my grandbabies, my friend, if instead I gave thanks for those people I loved so deeply, I felt better. The sadness would leave and in its place, the appreciation for my life grew. In most cases the love grew, connections deepened, and I discovered a great gift: love knows no borders, barriers, or conventional distinctions. Love is love is love. Let the active art of not missing give you its gift. I am so grateful.
© Science of Mind Magazine, September 2010
Rev. Barbara Leger

Since then, with help from my friends and more than a few therapy sessions, I came to see how my self-righteousness and the residual anger behind it didn't help anyone. It especially didn't serve me.

Not without difficulty, I began to "do the work" of healing. When I was feeling particularly sad or mad, and came to realize that there was nothing I could do about it right then, I looked around me and found something in my own life to be thankful for. There is always something, closer to home than you think, to be grateful for.

In difficult times try to get to the next best thought. Look around you. Find something to be glad for, even if it is that you are not somebody or somewhere else. Today, for me, it's the sun that has just broken through Monterey's thick drizzly fog earlier than usual this morning at 8:43 a.m. Today I am not in the cold Northeast, or a victim of a hurricane that flooded my house, or without heat or water. Today I am alive and well. Thank you, God!

In my workshops I ask participants to share at least three things they are glad to have in their lives, at that very moment. I also suggest they think of someone who, long ago, played an important role in their life, or did something that they would like to thank them for and suggest they actually find a way to do it. At the very least they can write an invisible letter. The energy of acknowledging gratitude goes a long way, even if not expressed in person.

Forgiveness is Not the Final Frontier

I took a workshop I found very useful at Omega Institute with Colin Tipping, whose books *Radical Forgiveness* and *Radical Self-forgiveness* and free Internet worksheets are available at www.colintipping.com. He helped me to say silently to myself or another person "I'm sorry this happened to you/me," while, at the same time, being grateful in some small way for part of it. He helped me to consider that "divine destiny" or "karma" might be operating in my situation.

At first it was difficult to swallow, that this heart-wrenching healing work I'd been doing, this book I was writing, may have been part of what I'm supposed to be doing on this planet this time around. No situation is perfect. Tipping helped me learn to honor my own *willingness* to go beyond my initial reaction, and do something with this that might help others.

Finally I began, as you have witnessed in the chronology of my letters, to be able to forgive not only Suzie, but also my ex and his wife Julie, and understand where they were coming from. I also learned to forgive myself for whatever "miss-take" I might have made in my parenting that could have contributed to this situation. I did the best I could do at the time, which is all any parent can do.

And Finally, Grandparent Yourself!

I end my workshops with Karen Drucker's song "Gentle With Myself "

I will be gentle with myself.
I will be gentle with myself.
And I will hold myself like a newborn baby child.

And I will only go as fast
as the slowest part of me feels safe to go.

And I rock myself like a newborn baby child.
I hold myself like a newborn baby child.
I love myself like a newborn baby child.

May we all take the time to rock ourselves, like the proverbial grandmother soothes a baby, in order to rise above whatever situation is in our face, and move on.

If separation of any kind haunts you, I suggest you grandmother yourself! We called my father's mother, "Ga Ga" when I was little, and later "Red" for her strawberry blonde hair. She was always there for me on a level my mother, sisters and even early husbands never were. As a child she took me to Broadway plays and lunches in places as wonderful as the Top of the Sixes in New York City. I could ask her anything and get straight answers.

At 25, when I returned at Christmas to my family after what I thought was a "simple divorce," I found myself crying all day long. My grandmother was the only one who not only acknowledged my tears, and she also comforted me by sharing stories from her two previous marriages. So, whether you are an invisible grandmother or auntie, or have some other separation in your life that is pressing, think of whispering things in your own ear that only a grandmother who unconditionally loves you could.

Recently I woke up after a dream with the words to a letter from my "Ga Ga" in my head. She'd be 114 now:

Dear Pattycakes,
You're doing a great job of Invisible Grandparenting.
Lighten up!
Your kids grew up in a loving home; you sat and
read to them, raised them to know right from wrong, to
value honesty and kindness, all that good stuff. You need
to know that at a certain age, perhaps any, your kids'
choices are not your fault! Forgive yourself. Remember
you did the best you could at the time.

Our kids come through us, they are not of us. Kahlil Gibran, remember?
And finally, you need to Grandmother yourself!
Go find something fun that you love to do and do it!
Love, Ga Ga
P.S. And I have a secret to tell you. Brad, now 32, is getting married in September to that girl he met on the mountain four years ago who first got him to re-contact his family. You may still get a chance to do the real thing!

The expression "time heals" is accurate in my case. I hope my story of this often-dark decade in my life will be an example that may help you find the light in your own. Take each day like it is a special birthday and give yourself special treats only an understanding grandmother could provide. Make every moment precious, now. You, too, can leave a legacy of love whether you can be there or not.

AN ELEVATED EPILOGUE

The wedding invitation I received confirmed my grandmother's message. Every time I looked at it I'd choke up. *"We consider China Peak one of our favorite places in the world. It's the place that we met, place where we have laughed, created many friendships and fell in love. China Peak is our special place and for that reason we want to share it with you. Our ceremony will be located at China Peak Mountain Resort at the Top of Chair 6. You get to take a chairlift ride to the top of the mountain! Yay!"* Call it a mother's tears of gladness, of relief, of joy or whatever, but I couldn't escape this being a pivotal point in my parenting journey.

Two days after the magic and beauty of my son's wedding, I am home. Down from the 8,000 feet mountain peak resort where Brad and his bride met four years ago, and I still feel elevated. Everything about the experience was "high." The sun was shining, it was eighty degrees with no humidity, and crystal clear piercing blue skies. The sheer rock and pines we viewed from the chairlift took our breath away.

My two movie-star gorgeous sons faced us from an altar of twisted wood and lace while Huntington Lake sparkled in the background. Silence fell over the crowd as the bride's Dad walked her down the aisle. I was honored to be part of the procession.

Taking both her hands in his, Brad locked eyes with his chosen one as together, they recited the simple vows they had written. The mountaintop rang out as the two of them repeated their lines with a conviction that left no doubt in anyone's mind: they meant what they were saying.

When it came time for the mother/son dance, Brad took me in his arms, and I looked up, took his face in my hands and told him "I've always loved you Brad, even when I didn't know where you were." He replied "me too." I even think I heard "I'm sorry for what I've put you through." I ended with congratulating him on finding such a fine woman. Then, as planned I signaled Julie to cut in. When she took over, I bowed to her, because really, she did the hard work of raising him every school year, I was just "Auntie Mame," remember? I truly was grateful for all the work she'd done and wanted to honor her.

Later, one of the photographers told me she had to put down the camera and wipe tears from her eyes during that dance. I guess the love I felt at that moment really showed. She remarked how utterly handsome both my boys were and said, "they look like you, not their father!" I was surprised; as a female it's hard to see a resemblance between my boys and me.

And here's the next surprise. During the last few years, I had put the prospect out of my mind that Brad would be a father again, and not only do it right, but "great" this time. Perhaps that's why I was startled at so many reminders of this possibility in my face. His bride's best friend introduced herself to me, as she was combing the blonde hair of her two daughters ages five and four that would be the flower girls! Another friend's six-year-old son was the ring bearer. A couple with two-month-old twins sat down at our table. A cousin of Brad's, that I've known since she was a child, was radiantly pregnant at 45. It was her first, with a new husband who looked much younger than her.

This post-wedding state I'm in feels like non-reality. It's as if I'm watching a movie with a happy ending; but I know this was very real. That handsome, high cheek-boned, clean-shaven young man in dress pants, vest and tie, who professed his love loudly, looking his equally gorgeous beautiful smiling bride in the eye, was my baby once. He was my teenager. Now as someone told me "he's all growed up." There was and still is, a palpable connection of love no matter the roads he'd dragged me down. "There he is," I realized, likely to start a family of his own!" Oh! My! God! Bless them.

So to my future grandchildren, who are still invisible and may at this moment be a swimming zygote of sperm and egg, "Before too long I may be able to do what I've been unable to all along: be a grandmother, a good and fully present one! I only hope it'll happen soon, before I've grown too old and feeble to enjoy it.

APPENDIX AND RESOURCES

⚀ ⚄ ⚀

AARP Foundation Grandparent Information Center (GIC)

The AARP Foundation Grandparenting Program's goal is to ensure that grandparents and grandchildren have access to resources that strengthen their health, finances and family connections. http://www.aarp.org/family/grandparenting/articles/grandparent_info_center.html

AARP's Grandcare Support Database

http://www.giclocalsupport.org/pages/gic_db_home.cfm
http://www.grandparentstoday

Advocates for Grandparent – Grandchild Connection, AFGGC

A 501(c)(3) non-profit, created on behalf of the children who have been denied access to their grandparents. It is a multigenerational organization that educates the public about grandparents' rights, advocates for grandchildren, and supports grandparents who have suffered from loss of affection and contact from their grandchildren. Executive Director Susan Hoffman's book and documentary film A Precious Bond: How to Preserve the Grandparent-Grandchild Relationship is a step by step guide to help grandparents right the wrongs that threaten the relationship is available at http://www.grandparentchildconnect.org/

Family Legal Help

Provides immediate access to grandparents rights attorneys lawyer in your local area who can tell you your grandparent's rights and options, and when feasible help you file for grandparent's custody or grandparent's visitation rights.
http://familylegalhelp.org/grandparents-rights

The Foundation For Grandparenting

A non-profit dedicated to raising Since 1980, is a non-profit dedicated to raising grandparent consciousness in order to better the lives of grandchildren, parents, grandparents, and communities through education, research, programs, communication, and networking. Its interactive website is devoted to fostering grandparent education, networking, research, and programs. http://www.grandparenting.org.

Grandparents Action Group (UK)

A non-profit group, run by volunteers to help maintain and protect the relationship between grandparents and grandchildren when contact has been denied or prevented. They campaign through Parliament for reforms to the current family law system. http://homepage.ntlworld.com/darkpowers/gagindex.htm

Legal Information for Families Today (LIFT)

http://www.liftonline.org/mission.html empowers families to advocate for themselves in the complex Family Courts and addresses the emotional ramifications of Court involvement. The mission of Legal Information for Families Today (LIFT) is to enhance access to justice for children and families by providing legal information, community education, and compassionate guidance, while promoting system-wide reform of the courts and public agencies.

Foster Grandparenting

Foster Grandparents are role models, mentors, and friends to children with exceptional needs. The program provides a way for volunteers age 55 and over to stay active by serving children and youth in their communities. http://www.nationalservice.gov/programs/senior-corps/foster-grandparents

Online Discussion Groups

Grandparenting: Joys&Challenges

http://www.aarp.org/online-community/groups/index.
action?slGroupKey=Group23892

Visitation with Grandchildren

http://www.aarp.org/online-community/groups/index.
action?slGroupKey=Group1862

Grandparents Unplugged

http://community.grandparents.com/index.php/forum/7-
grandparents-unplugged/

Grandparents Without Grandchildren

http://community.grandparents.com/index.php/forum/8-
grandparents-without-grandchildren/

Grandparenting from Afar

http://community.grandparents.com/index.php/forum/14-
grandparenting-from-afar/

Made in the USA
San Bernardino, CA
21 October 2013